The Household Library of Exposition.

THE LORD'S PRAYER.

THE
LORD'S PRAYER

BY
CHARLES STANFORD, D.D.,

WIPF & STOCK · Eugene, Oregon

Wipf and Stock Publishers
199 W 8th Ave, Suite 3
Eugene, OR 97401

The Lord's Prayer
By Stanford, Charles
Softcover ISBN-13: 978-1-7252-9786-9
Hardcover ISBN-13: 978-1-7252-9788-3
eBook ISBN-13: 978-1-7252-9787-6
Publication date 1/20/2021
Previously published by Macmillan & Co., 1883

This edition is a scanned facsimile of
the original edition published in 1883.

PREFACE.

THE following homilies were in substance first preached in the ordinary course of the author's ministry, and have since been written out from rough notes, or from memory. In November 1881, while engaged in thus getting them ready for the press, it became needful for him to consult an oculist, and his sentence was, "*Glaucoma:* fast fading sight." In consequence of this, much of the manuscript has been written by him with shut eyes, and much set down at his dictation by the hand that has helped him in all other things.

"All is said, and we come too late."* Nearly two centuries are gone since this remark was penned; and if it had some truth in it then, how much more now, especially as to the great subject of this small book!

The same argument for silence would, how-

* Jean de la Bruyère.

ever, have equal strength against the discussion of any other vital subject of Christian truth or duty, and although the Lord's Prayer has already been so fully discussed by men of the highest worth, even now, any Christian who, as in this instance, utters his own living thoughts about it, in his own natural way, and with a simple wish to honour God, may hope thus to be of some service to his fellow Christians. May this grace be given.

CHARLES STANFORD.

CAMBERWELL, *April* 1883.

CONTENTS.

CHAP		PAGE
I.	JESUS, THE TEACHER OF PRAYER	1
	"Lord, teach us to pray"	
II.	THE LORD'S PRAYER GIVEN AS A PATTERN	29
	"After this manner therefore pray ye"	
III.	THE INVOCATION	53
	"Our Father which art in heaven"	
IV.	THE FIRST PETITION	84
	"Hallowed be Thy Name."	
V.	THE SECOND PETITION	112
	"Thy kingdom come."	
VI.	THE THIRD PETITION	130
	"Thy will be done in earth"	
VII.	THE FOURTH PETITION	156
	"Give us our daily bread."	

CHAP		PAGE
VIII. THE FIFTH PETITION	. . . .	179
	"Forgive us our debts"	
IX. THE SIXTH PETITION	. . . .	203
	"Lead us not into temptation."	
X. THE SEVENTH PETITION	. . . .	229
	"Deliver us from evil"	

I.

JESUS, THE TEACHER OF PRAYER.

"Lord, teach us to pray."—LUKE xi. 1. (*Authorized and* (*Revised Version.*

THIS discourse is simply introductory. Only in the smallest degree does it profess to offer notes on any passage in the Lord's Prayer, or on any of its historical circumstances; yet it is hoped that, by the blessing of the Highest, it may help to tune some spirits for the thoughts that follow, and waken some hearts into sympathy with the lessons that Christ is about to teach, by showing from the Scriptures in general, these two things:—

I. Why Jesus is to be regarded as the Teacher of prayer.

II. How He teaches.

I. We have to show *why Jesus is to be regarded as the Teacher of Prayer?*

It should be taken for granted that knowing how to pray is the first of all essentials. Men may know, or think they know, how to discuss questions of Divine metaphysics, and may talk as if they thought themselves "privy councillors to the King of kings," but, after all, without a knowledge of prayer, they have only a knowledge of surfaces. God is still a secret; a veil hides the mercy seat, and though they may claim to know all about the cabinet of Gospel truth, with all its treasury of things "new and old," they only know the outside of it; the door is locked, and there is no key. Yet no one need "perish for lack of this knowledge." If we want information, we may have it.

There was once a man in Palestine who said that He was the Son of God, and what He did, proved that what He said was true. Of Him it was written by the pen of the Holy Ghost, " No man hath seen God at any time; the only begotten Son, who is in the bosom of the Father, He hath declared Him." When He had lived the three years which made visible the eternity of unseen Divine love, had spoken out the simple, great, creative words of eternal life, and had wrought out, by the sacrifice of Himself, the one plan for restoring the bond which sin had broken between the Maker and the made, He carried our nature alive and uninjured right through the death of the cross,—still in the body, though changed into a body of glory; He then went up into the throne of mediation, and there He ever lives to bestow what here He died to procure.

When we would know how to pray, we, like

the first disciples, think that if anyone can tell us, He can. It is plain from the sequel to their request, that they were not only right in making it, but right in making it to Him, and that we therefore shall be right in repeating it. He is the Teacher of prayer. This is His business. Now He is ascended, His disciples are always learning to pray, and He is always teaching.

No! some will say, this teaching is the province, not of the Son, but of the Holy Ghost. But not a single instance do we find in all the New Testament of a request for instruction made to the Holy Ghost. It is not to the Spirit that disciples may go with the petition—"Lord, teach us to pray." In all our approaches to the Infinite Unseen, we have first to do with Jesus; every prayer must reach His ear before we have the answer to it; like Stephen, like Paul, like those who followed Him during His earthly life, it is still our delightful right to speak out all our fears, all our cares, and all our questions, to Him as to our present Lord, with this difference only—that He is not with us as He was with them, veiled in a human form.*
When we speak to Him, we speak to the Spirit, for the Spirit is in Him, and in Him as the

* That human form, having answered the ends for which it was taken, would, if still retained on earth, be but a veil before His divine glory, διὰ τοῦ καταπετάσματος, τοῦτ' ἔστι, τῆς σαρκὸς αὐτοῦ.—Heb. x. 20.

Head of the Church, that He may give out holy influences. It is as much as ever one of His functions and part of His work as our Saviour to be the Teacher of prayer, and He teaches by the agency of the Spirit—of the Spirit of whom it is written—"He shall not speak of Himself, He shall glorify Me." "It is the Spirit that quickeneth." "The Spirit helpeth our infirmities, for we know not how to pray as we ought, but the Spirit Himself maketh intercession for us with groanings which cannot be uttered, and He that searcheth the heart, knoweth what is the mind of the Spirit, because He maketh intercession for the saints according to the will of God."*

II. Next, let us enquire *how He teaches*. We must distinguish between agency and instrumentality. The agent is One—that is, Jesus, by the Holy Spirit's influence; the instruments are many—and we now propose to glance at some of the many instruments through which this influence works, in order that we may answer the question before us.

1. He sometimes begins to teach us by means of *an overheard prayer*. The first necessity in the process of teaching us is, that there should be roused in us the wish to learn. The sinner never anticipates the Saviour. He begins to teach before we begin to ask Him, and it is

* Rom. viii. 26, 27 (*Revised Version*).

JESUS, THE TEACHER OF PRAYER. 5

at His own mystic prompting that we pray to be taught. The instrument of this prompting is frequently an overheard prayer. It was so in the chapter of events to which the text belongs.

"And it came to pass that, as He was praying in a certain place," I think it was in secret, "when He ceased, one of His disciples said unto Him, Lord, teach us to pray."

John Bunyan, telling the story of his pilgrims, says in one passage, "Now, when they were almost at the end of the ground, they perceived that a little before them was a solemn noise as of one that was much concerned. So they went on, and looked before them, and behold they saw, as they thought, a man upon his knees, with his hands and eyes lift up, and speaking, as they thought, earnestly to one that was above. They drew nigh, but could not tell what he said, so they went softly till he had done. When he had done, he got up, and began to run towards the Celestial City."

If I read aright the short notes that Luke has left us, the disciples, on the occasion here notified, overheard the secret prayers of God's Holy One! The deep impression left on me is, that there was not only something extraordinary in the prayer itself, but in the circumstance that they heard it—that it was not a family prayer, such as, doubtless, they had already many a time heard Him utter, and in which they had taken part, but one in which they could not take part, and with which mortals could have nothing to do—one in which He was terribly alone, gloriously alone—one which made them feel that they had never prayed before, and had now to begin learning. If, in old time, a man without meaning it had overheard the secret prayer of Jacob, when, under the stars, he wrestled with the "Traveller Unknown;" if a man had overheard that prayer of Elijah which shut the heavens; or that which, three years after, opened them again; if a man had overheard the prayer of Daniel in the night when he was left with the tremendous lions; if a man had lost himself in the Temple, and had somehow got shut within the curtains of the Holy Place, so that he oversaw the secret glory flame out, and overheard the secret, lonely priest pray—what would such overhearings have been in comparison with this! No seer has told us how it came to pass, but our minds seem just now to have a vision of it. Jesus has been praying in the mountain all night. In the morning His disciples go out to meet Him as He comes down. They are pushing up through the dewy leaves, and round by the boulders, when—hush!

There, in "a certain place," is Jesus, praying. Suddenly they feel as if they had been caught up into the third heaven, and were hearing "unspeakable words, not lawful for man to utter." It seems to them that they have no right to be there, and they try to step softly away, but a power, not their own, holds them like a hand, and with a fearful joy their thrilled and lifted spirits hear the prayer all through. "Whether in the body or out of the body," whether rich or poor, whether in trouble or in joy, they cannot tell. They are carried quite out of themselves. Jesus is not in their world. We read that when He ceased, "one of the disciples said, Lord, teach us to pray." *

No wonder! Such a prayer as that will never more be heard on this our star. We must die before we can see the face of Jesus, as He now is, or hear His voice like "the sound of glory ringing in our ears." But we still have his spiritual presence, and in a great sense He is still on earth incarnate—incarnate by His grace—incarnate now not in one form only, but in millions. His Spirit being still with us, still we may hear Him pray through human lips.

Among the many surprises by which He

* In speaking of the prayer overheard by the disciples, as one of our great Intercessor's own solitary prayers, the preacher only presumes to give his own view of what was probable. Of course, others have an equal right to make a different statement, but no one must speak with positiveness.

wakes in us the wish to pray, such an overheard prayer is still one. Some of you can bear witness to this. There is a man whose first wish to pray was prompted by the praying life of his mother. There is a man, a father in Israel now, whose first wish to pray was prompted by the overheard prayers of an old farm servant, as he knelt amidst corn-sacks and under cob-webbed rafters, yet as before the lone Majesty of majesty. There is a man whose first wish to pray was prompted by the overheard prayers of his own little child. "Little children," we have been told by a great sage, "are professors in Christ's college." Sometimes, when you open the book of wonderful things, intending to teach your child, he will suddenly teach you. Sometimes he will ask you precisely the right questions—the next thing to knowing precisely the right answers. Sometimes he will pierce the centre of some great truth with startling ease and directness; and sometimes while he is talking to his Heavenly Father with artless, fearless faith, and with quaint, loving prattle, adding a prayer of his own to that he has been taught to say—he makes you, old Christian as you are, ashamed to find how much you have to learn, and how far you are from the secret place of the Most High. Though there may for the moment be a smile on the lip, there will be a tear in the eye and a prayer in the heart, making the words leap out almost before you are aware, "Lord, teach me to pray."

2. Jesus teaches us to pray by *our troubles*. "Head over all things to the church," one function of His meditating love is to rule and sanctify events, sending through them to human hearts the memories of His truth and the forces of His Spirit. In this part of His saving work it is His way to use trouble as an incitement to prayer, and so teaches how to pray. We shall not be understood to mean that every cry to God in trouble is an outforce of Christ's teaching Spirit. In many an instance such a cry is only instinctive, like the cry of the sea birds in a storm.

> "There is no God," the foolish saith;
> But none, "there is no sorrow,"
> And Nature, oft the cry of Faith,
> In bitter need will borrow.

"Nature in an agony is no atheist." Once, in a case known to me, a man who had argued himself into the most self-complacent materialism had a great affliction; the blow broke him down; nature was too strong for his mere theories, and looking round on the silent company of those who had come to comfort him, he said, "perhaps there is a God—somewhere—pray, somebody!" Once, a man whose very name had passed into a proverb of sarcastic infidelity, when in a crisis of trouble, cried, "O

God, have mercy!" This was no new thing in the history of souls. Five hundred years before the words " Lord, teach us to pray " were spoken, a poet penned this similar story,—" When the Grecian forces hotly pursued our host, and we must need venture over the great river Strymon, frozen then, but beginning to thaw, and a hundred to one we had all died for that thaw, with my own eyes I saw many of those gallants whom I had heard before so boldly maintain there was no God, everyone upon his knees and devoutly praying that the ice might hold till they got over."

Perhaps before the Son of God came into this world as the Son of man, He did by virtue of His yet unrevealed expiation, and by the influence of His mysterious spirit, not yet formally inaugurated, speak to men in times of the power, or of the tender listening sensibility, or of the yearning after God, incited by trouble, and by means of this trouble began to strive with them, thus in some degree teaching them to pray. We know He does so now. Almost all our Ebenezers have been set up, like the memorable one of old, in some place out of which trouble compelled us to cry for help, and in the acute instant of that cry we said our first lesson. After a time of terror, John Newton wrote, "About this time I began to know that there is a God who hears and answers prayer."* After

Letter to Rev. Mr Haweis, January 19, 1763.

such a time you might make the like memorandum. The time when the soul seems to be slipping off some cliff of life, or going over the pitch of some dread Niagara, or the time when all standing ground seems about to open, or the time when going down to "do business in deep waters," your ship seems about to split—such is often the agony point of time when the soul is surprised into its first prayer. There is beautiful order in the very hurricane of trial, and the calm Jesus is in the very heart of the cyclone teaching that prayer. The moment of love unspeakable, intolerable, alone; the moment when, thrilling at the touch of a clay hand, or the sight of a dim, still face, done with time; the moment when the heart was weak as a breaking wave, and all the world seemed to snap like a touched bubble, when all the use seemed to die out of you, and yet you had to live somehow, was the moment perhaps when you first felt a prayer moving within you. It came without any call of yours, but in truth it was the Saviour talking in your heart, and teaching you to pray. Sad to say, after such an initial moment, and when a praying life has been startled into existence, that life will have its fits of apathy or levity, making it needful that it should be startled again. The levity of the Londoners in old time, whose churches were full during the scaring visits of the plague, but empty when it was gone, originated the proverb now long out of use, "No prayer, no paternoster." In the spring of the year 1588, when the Spanish Armada was expected, all England seemed to be alive with prayer, and, says an old annalist, "it might have been written in golden letters over the door of every sanctuary in the land, *cor unum, via una;* but when the fear was over, and the year grew old, the prayers grew cold." Do such public facts seem to have their reflections in the facts of our own secret history? Are we, with all our evangelical daylight, dull to God as were the people of the Gothic ages? Are we such unconscious materialists that we only have a life of spiritual intensity and realising prayer when terror knocks us down, or when trouble desolates our outward lot? Must it be said of us, "Lord, in trouble they have visited Thee," "They poured out a prayer when Thy chastening was upon them;" and must we add the life of prayer began to droop with the return of prosperity? Then we shall have to find that "trials give new life to prayer." The Lord will repeat the lesson. Somehow we must learn it, and if we will learn by no other way, it must be by trouble. This principle will account for many a dispensation that we have been accustomed to call mysterious. If we can find no other reason for it, we can almost always find this one, that it makes us pray. When the elements of true piety, which are the elements of true prayer, have become hardened in a worldly atmosphere, they are brought into fusion again by the fire of adversity, all your glowing soul is "melted within you because of trouble," and flows forth to God; and what is this but a process by which Christ is teaching you to pray?

Old English divines, in homely dramatic fashion, sometimes used a certain passage in Old Testament story as a parable to expound how the Lord of our dull reluctant spirits makes them pray. A certain Eastern prince once rode up to a certain farmer's gate and said, "Come out, I would speak with thee!" The farmer took no notice. Again the prince cried out, "Come out!" There was still no notice. "Come out!" he shouted; and when there was still no notice taken of his call, he flung a lighted brand over the gate into the dry, rustling barley. Then the man (his name was Joab) came out and said, "Wherefore hast thou set my barley-field on fire?" The reason was not far to fetch, the prince had thus gained his end, and had got the sullen man out for an interview. We may question the taste of this apologue, and say that it is almost an act of irreverence to weave out from the fact of a man's fury a lesson of God's love; but, at least, no one can mistake its point, and no one can deny its truth. No doubt, when we will not consent to an interview, man alone with God alone, God often lights up a great fire of affliction. He makes "burning instead of beauty." He begins to burn down some "dear delight" that we would most fondly cherish, or some possession that we had set our hearts upon; then we, who had shut ourselves up from Him, come out; we who had dropped into a habit of indolence, and had become unwilling to offer energetic prayer, are stirred to pray at last; and it may be said of the disciple whose praying life, long declining, is thus quickened by trouble, as was said in an ancient poem of a certain hero in trouble, "Out of his heart there poured a mighty cry." So the Lord teaches us to pray.

3. Jesus teaches prayer *by revealing Himself as the one medium of prayer*. This He does, first by the letter, next by the spirit of His instructions. By the letter, we mean the language. If we would know the Christian theory of sin, and the Christian conception of prayer, we go to the Fountain-head, and ponder the language of Him in whom all Christian life begins. He says to us at once, "I am the way, and the truth, and the life, no man cometh to the Father but by Me." "Whatsoever ye shall ask the Father in My name, that will I do, that the Father may be glorified in the Son." All His other instructions are built on these lines.

When we enter His school, the school-book which He puts into our hands has, for its central peculiarity, the doctrine that He is the one avenue by which a sinner's prayers reach God, and that He is so by virtue of His atoning sacrifice. This principle of our acceptance through Him is awfully told in the word "blood" —the "red word"—the word which we would only utter with a tremble of reverence—the word which spoken lightly in our hearing, even by a preacher, makes a hush in our spirits, a wish to cover our faces, and a fear that would cry "Holy, holy, holy!" This word meets us in almost every page of the law, and is as much to be seen in the plain statements of the New Testament as in the typical pictures of the Old. If we have fellowship with Him who is "the Light," "the blood of Jesus Christ His Son cleanseth us from all sin;" if we would "draw nigh to God," we "draw nigh by the blood of Christ;" if "we have boldness to enter into the holiest," it is "by the blood of Jesus, by the new and living way."

We are told by doubters of the Atonement that this is only poetry, and that the "blood of Jesus Christ" is only a phrase used to give out the general idea that Jesus Christ does in some way cleanse the soul and make it holy. But this is no mere poetry! Poetry takes its laws from Nature. Poetry delights in the beautiful;

does Nature suggest the imagery of Leviticus? Is blood beautiful? Does blood in the battle-field make that which it washes whiter than snow? Sprinkled on the golden mercy-seat of old, did it make the gold flash? or on the book, did it make its leaves clean? or on the vessels of the sanctuary, did it take out the stains of service? Is not its red, wet mark, a foul thing? and do not men sometimes turn sick, faint, and dark at the sight of it? Mere man's poetry of purity never created this emblem. Poetry made the murderess in Macbeth look at her hand, shiver, and cry as against the intolerable— "Out, damned spot! Out, I say! One, two, . . . There's the smell of the blood still! All the perfumes of Arabia will not sweeten this little hand. Oh, oh, oh!" If poetry had selected a symbol of cleansing, the symbol would not have been blood, but water. Water is the universal solvent, purity making purity; the crystal beauty, beauty. Used by the Only Wise as a word for teaching lost souls the way back home, it must point to sacrificial cleansing, and its use all through the Bible would confound our reason unless as the sign for sacrifice. Once an inspired interpreter speaking of the blood that his hearers were looking at, when in attendance at the Temple services said, "The blood is the life!" How? He must have meant life not *in* the body, but *out* of it; life which, being then out of the body, implied the death of the body—"a life laid down." Jesus, fulfilling the words, "I lay down my life for the sheep," fulfilled the typical meaning of "the blood." The blood "shed," or "poured out," or, "offered in sacrifice," was his very *life*, "shed," or "poured out," or "offered in sacrifice," life for life. In the Divine plan of things, it is only for the sake of this offering, that the sinner, and so the sinner's prayers, can be acceptable.

Pleading this, though once banished out of sight and speech from God as his Father, he may now "come with boldness to the throne of grace." Doubtless the Atonement has endless aspects heavenward and earthward, and glorious ramifications of meaning that open into infinity. It is not to be supposed that the few proof texts that we are accustomed to quote—precious as they are as exquisite definitions, short summaries, or watch-words of telling brevity, were ever intended to exhaust or explain the whole wonder; but many of these, while they say little about its influence beyond our immediate necessity for it, and nothing about reasons, state the plan of the Gospel with such plainness, that the simplest child in the nursery, or the poorest man at the crossing, may understand enough of it to rest all his weight on it and be saved-- enough to use it as that which shall surely carry his prayers up into heaven—enough for practical purpose—enough for the present, all that there is now time for. You may have the teaching of the latter to perfection, yet be far from mastering the secret of acceptable prayer. It is the *heart* that must pray; the heart must be the real scholar. When Christ teaches, it is the heart that is the critic; the heart that rebels. Out of the heart comes the voice that cries— Why should prayer by way of Christ's sacrifice be the standing order of salvation? Why should I come to God this way? Why will not another way do as well? If I come somehow, what does it matter how? It is the heart that infects the conviction of the intellect; but sometimes, when the creed of the intellect is that of the Epistle to the Romans, the creed of the heart may be heathen, and under words of Christian truth there may slumber the hope of being heard, not as a sinner by the rights of Christ, but by virtue of some right thing of your own. In a recent voyage an iron gun was in such a position on board that it drew aside the needle of the compass, and kept it from pointing quite truly; the effect was, that, spite of skilful seamanship, the ship nearly ran upon a rock. Owing to the iron in the heart, conscience, the compass of the soul, will often deviate, and your prayer may get into a wrong course. Christ can change that iron, and so practically teach you the right. Each tried Christian is a

JESUS, THE TEACHER OF PRAYER. 19

witness to this. More than one who listens to me now might make the confession, Long after I had thought myself a Christian, I failed to appreciate the mediatorial element in the groundwork of prayer, and there was a certain slight of Christ in my habits of devotion, then, by the Holy Spirit, who comes in the name and place of Christ, and whose province is, not to speak of Himself, but to take of the things of Christ and show them to us, Christ taught my heart, dissolving my doubts, melting my pride, charming me into sympathy with His own way of saving me, and inspiring in me a spirit of total surrender, until I could say, "Jesus, I see it all now, it is all beautifully right. Thou hast undertaken my cause for me. Joyfully do I give up to Thee, and live in Thee. In Thee I appear before God in prayer, in Thee I stand accepted."

4. Jesus teaches us to pray *by making His own Spirit the spirit of our lives.* That indwelling Spirit will make your life a prayer, so that praying words will become only some of its natural expressions. The most loving Christians, however, have their dull seasons, when the soul is sadly under-vitalized, and has to cry, " I cleave to the dust, quicken me, according to Thy Word."

Then, prayers seem like dead things. The suppliant has thought of the right petitions, and given them the right shape, but seems unable to give them wing. There is an ancient story about Christ's childhood to the effect that, one day when He was with other children, they, in their play, made some clay into the shape of birds, and that the child Jesus gave life to these clay birds, making them fly.

My prayer-bird was cold—would not away,
Although I set it on the edge of the nest.
Then I bethought me of the story old—
Love-fact, or loving fable, thou knowest best—
How, when the children had made sparrows of clay,
Thou mad'st them birds, with wings to flutter and fold;
Take, Lord, my prayer in Thy hand, and make it pray.

So sings George Macdonald, although he has not yet given his song to the world. "Beautiful!" we cry. When we have shaped our prayers—and yet, somehow they will not rise—let us offer the words over again, and wait on Him who is our life, to breathe Himself into them and give them wing; only let us never forget that, first or last, the life He puts into our prayers He first puts into us. He makes them alive, by first making us alive, and so teaches us to pray.

As we speak, a recollection strikes us of certain vivid words of His which compel us to change our metaphor, but only to get another aspect and a yet happier conception of the same truth. Talking to the Woman of Samaria, He said, "Whosoever shall drink of the water that I shall give him, shall never thirst, but the water that I shall give him *shall be in him a well of water springing* up into everlasting life." This may help to account for a common phenomenon of the Christian's inward life. He may say, sometimes, without meaning it, without a thought beforehand, and occasionally even without words, Amidst the activities of the day, and when I wake in the night, I find myself speaking to God; I have hopes, fears, yearnings, hurries of feeling Godwards; all my life seems to turn and tremble that way, waves of prayer seem to throb and swell in my soul. What is the meaning of all this? I know it is Jesus, teaching me to pray, and this commotion within me is the "well of water" that He gives "springing up into everlasting life." Did you ever stop to trace the beginning of a river? Down in the solitude, in the dimness, amidst the tangled roots of things, under the grass, the water springs and palpitates, breaks up through ferns and mosses, bubbles into beauty, leaps and lightens, darkles and sparkles, wells and swells, bursts through all obstacles, works up through the sand, will find a way out into the sunshine, till that which began in secret becomes a broad and tranquil river helping to carry the fleets of nations and to make the boundaries of empire. So the water that Christ gives us is "in us a well of water springing up." In mysterious intuitions, stirs of life, sanctities of feeling, and longings after the Infinite, it springs and springs, works and works, down amidst broken stones, in the tangle, in the heart, in the dark, in the secrecy which only the eye of God can search. These mystic movements in me, inclining me Godwards, seem to show that Jesus has me in hand, that He has begun the good work in me, and is teaching me to pray. Work in me mightily, Spirit of Jesus, "spring up, O well!"

5. Jesus teaches to pray by *quickening the sense* of difficulty. Paley has told us that when he was a college tutor he found it easy to make his pupils understand the solution of a thing; the difficulty was to make them alive to the difficulty. The same principle works in every kind of learning, human and Divine. In learning prayer, unless you have a sense of difficulty, you will not make much way. Jesus, by His Spirit, gives the praying power; by difficulty, He educates it.

Unhappily, the notion is everywhere afloat that prayer, though a good and holy thing, is something dreamy, something wordy, something easy, something for women, children, ministers, and other good people who have no more knowledge than is necessary, and who have nothing to do. It may be hard to master a language, they think, hard to see through a science; hard to study, hard to preach, hard to practise, but it must be easy to pray. A distinction is made between working and praying, and it is understood that praying is not working. The man of the world says, "Work is worship;" we say, "Worship is work."

One great difficulty is *realising God*. It may be easy to kneel, easy to speak, but it is not easy to feel with all the life of reality that there is in the silence a listening; in the vacancy a power; and so to keep up a real and effective communication between the Spirit and the Father of spirits. Once this realization might not have troubled you much, but since you have been trying to pray in good earnest under the direction of Christ, there are moments when you feel that it makes even a torment of difficulty.

Another difficulty is the frequent *coldness of desire Godward*. The simple Christians of Labrador said to the Moravian missionaries, "We wish to have such a longing after God as a child has towards its mother, or as a man in the chase has for the reindeer." This coldness of heavenly desire had never been felt a difficulty in the way of their prayers to their old heathen gods; it was altogether a new sense, quickened into existence by their new Lord and Master. Our experience is often a similar sorrowful sense of check and incapacity arising from spiritual coldness.

Another difficulty, and one much felt by Christian men amidst the hard work and keen competitions of modern life, is *the effect on their souls of the atmosphere in which they have to live*, making it on many occasions, even when they try to pray, long before they can fix thought, or burn with a praying spirit. Even our leisurely ancestors felt it. "Our thoughts," wrote one of them, "are like green sticks lying on the fire, sobbing and smoking long before they burst into a blaze." It is Christ who makes us fret and chafe at this "power of the air" on our souls, seeming to saturate and damp them so that prayer will not burn. This gave us no trouble before we knew Him.

Another difficulty is from *vain thoughts*. "If," said Philip Henry, "our prayers were written down and our vain thoughts interlined, what nonsense there would be!" Vain thoughts were not counted amongst the difficulties of life, before Christ began to teach him prayer.

A kindred difficulty is the *restlessness* we often feel in the act of prayer. Every one of us can understand the entry made by homely William Smith of Coalville, in the diary of his soul, "While at prayer my mind was rather shifting. I had to bring it back *and ask it to sit down*." *
We are baffled and weighted by ignorance, by infirmity and by countless things, which to-

* "Hanani," Dr Grosart, p. 52.

gether make such a total that we feel inclined
to think with Coleridge that "the act of praying,
in its most perfect form, is the very highest
energy of which the human mind is capable."
The difficulty does not begin when we begin to
pray under the teaching of Christ, but the *sense*
of it does; and this He uses for carrying on His
purpose. When you have made acquaintance
with a thing through difficulties you are more
sure of your ground. Altogether, your knowledge has more depth and your practice more
facility than it could have had in any other way.
By quickening the sense of difficulty the Angel
wrestles us into strength, and teaches the
suppliant to say, " I will not let Thee go except
Thou bless me."

In these, and in other ways, Jesus teaches
prayer. It is remarkable that He only teaches
prayer, never the *philosophy* of prayer. The
sentiment of not a few appears to be, that this
philosophy is the very thing that we first have
to learn. The first questions, even of Christians,
are too often simply speculative ; and in almost
every one of the many treatises on prayer they
have given to the world in recent years, a large
space is taken up with the discussion of such
questions. More than they are aware, they are
influenced in this direction by the spirit of the
times. Each young believer is now likely to be
brought more or less in contact with some

theorist who owns no higher teacher of religion than science, who smiles down upon him, assures him that the discoveries of science prove the alleged power of prayer to be impossible; and says, "It is useless for you to expect that the laws of nature will be set aside because you pray!"

"Who wants the laws of nature to be set aside?" might be the reply. "Assuredly I do not. I know very little about the laws of nature, and even you know very little more. For aught your science can show, it may be quite possible for God to answer prayers, without in the least degree touching the settled constitution of the universe."

Our conviction is that we find wrought into our very nature, as one of its primary principles, the instinct that prompts to prayer. We find in the Bible a renewal of this law, together with directions, incentives, and promises encouraging our obedience to it. On evidence that satisfies our reason, we believe the Bible to be as much the word, as creation is the work of God. Then, as a matter of course, our common sense refuses to believe that when He "who seeth the end from the beginning," made the world, He shut Himself out of it, establishing such fixed and strong arrangements that they have totally mastered Him, so that although He has promised to hear our prayers, He is in the position of one who has to say—I am sorry, very sorry, but circumstances quite unforeseen, and entirely beyond my control, have now made me unable to keep my word! When, therefore, the Nebuchadnezzar of modern opinion demands that we shall answer all his questions before we pray, and that we shall bow down before the golden theories that he has set up, on pain of being cast into "the burning, fiery furnace" of his contempt, we say what the three confessors said to the royal dogmatist of old, "O king, we are not careful to answer thee in this matter!"

We would yield to none in enthusiasm for the study of natural science, nor in our admiration of those who are working out the process of its endless and fascinating discoveries. Only what is false in faith can depend on what is false in science. Every truth must be consistent with every other truth in the universe of God. Sure as that there is truth in the doctrine of prayer, the power of prayer must be in harmony with the reign of law; the efficacy of the one with the stability of the other. These are our convictions. Up to this time, however, we are not entirely satisfied with any solutions of the problem in question. Perhaps we shall find one, some when and some where; but we think not. in this short and germinal stage of existence. Some day in the infinite future, He who is the sole Master in this school, may grant some of these explanations that naturalists ask for so eagerly that he may or may not do. We see no reason why he should. As we take food and get nourishment from it, before we can understand the philosophy of nutrition; as we think before we can understand the laws of thought, and move before we can understand all the mysteries of motion ; so we may realize all the advantages of prayer before we can understand its place in the system of the universe, and in the counsels by which the universe is swayed. If a truth be *ascertained*, and the mind of the man who knows it be healthy, no dark things connected with the philosophy of it will disturb his faith. Knowing, as a matter of fact, that God is the hearer of prayer, we shall not be stopped in our prayers by arguments drawn from theoretic difficulties. It is enough for the present that Jesus teaches the practice of prayer ; we can wait for knowledge of the philosophy.

II.

THE LORD'S PRAYER GIVEN AS A PATTERN.

"After this manner therefore pray ye."—MATT. vi. 10.
"When ye pray say . . ."—LUKE xi. 2.
Authorized and Revised Version.

THE writer of the Epistle to the Hebrews says, "Moses was admonished by God when he was about to build the Tabernacle, for, see, saith He, that thou make all things according to *the pattern* shewed thee on the mount."* We venture to borrow this phrase. When the disciples said, "Lord, teach us to pray," the prayer that we are now reading was shown as a pattern. Here, we have a ground plan to fill in, and on whose lines we may build the structure of our petitions every time we pray.

I. Observe, *it is not one of our Lord's own prayers* that is given for a pattern. This we think is what the inquirers mainly meant and asked for. When the sound of His prayer was over, their thought was, "well, this is prayer indeed, would that we could pray just like it— Lord, teach us!"

* Hebrews viii. 5.

Many crude and random words are now in the air about Christ as our pattern. "A Christian is one who aims to take Christ as his pattern in everything, is he not?" When a secularist asks you this question, you are apt at once to say "Yes," for what is thus spoken, so rings like a truth, and so looks like a first principle, that you let it pass without a challenge. He has you now. Then he proceeds to argue that, if all Christians said and did exactly similar things to those which the four gospels report Christ to have said and done, they would dissolve society, and the world would be no place for us to live in. Thus he works out the conclusion that no one is, no one ever can be, a thorough Christian, and goes on to prove, as he thinks, that the creed of Christianity is untrue because the practice of it would be impossible.

There is an error in the seemingly indisputable statement that a Christian is in all respects to copy Christ. In the great Puritan allegory, one old pilgrim, reviewing his life as he stands at the brink of the river, is reported to have said, "I have loved to hear my Lord spoken of, and whenever I have seen the print of His shoe in the earth, there I have coveted to set my foot too." His words make an echo in my heart, yet they can only be mine with an important element of reserve. I see the foot-

GIVEN AS A PATTERN.

mark of my Lord in places where it would be proud profanity for me to try and "set my shoe." As my Prophet, Priest, and King; as the Sinless One; as the Searcher of hearts; as the Revealer of truth; as the Judge of all the earth, who is always right,—He had to step where it would be death for me to venture; and this was not only in the path of action but in the path of prayer.

See Him at nightfall, as, amidst the gloom that wavers and the mist that clings,—when the birds are still, and man is dropping his weary head upon the pillow,—He walks with grass-muffled feet up the steep cleft, through the trees, out into the open at the mountain top, the peaceful infinite above, the white world below—there to be alone with the Father. May I go up into that holiest place with Him, and can I dare to tread in the print of His feet? Is prayer like that which He is breathing any rule for me? Am I, though His follower, bound thus to spend my nights? Surely I must not be in despair because this is impossible; I have not His cup to drink, His Calvary to climb. He walked through sublime passages of prayer, not as a sinner such as I am, but as the Saviour of sinners; He prayed as the Son of God, who, in His adopted nature as the Son of man, had but three years in which to accomplish His awful minisrty. From the first, only what looked like a little moment lay between Him and Gethsemane; He was always under the shadow of that cross on which He had to know the utmost secrets of agony, and on the efficacy of which all salvation depended; no wonder that He spent long nights in prayer. You might as well ask me to walk the waves like Christ, to heal the sick like Christ, to raise the dead like Christ, or to die on the altar of sacrifice like Christ, as to pray like Christ. Besides, being alone in His intercessions as the Saviour, He was alone as the perfect man. He had no sin to confess, no pardon to implore; He never joined in saying "Our Father," but when speaking to His disciples about God, made the careful distinction, "Your Father and My Father. Your God and My God." There must have been secrets in His communion with which no stranger could intermeddle, and thoughts as much beyond our comprehension as His work is beyond our power. We are to be like Christ, not in doing the like deeds, or in saying the like words, but in having the like Spirit, animating us in the infinitely different offices we have to fill, and works we have to do as saved sinners. It is out of the question that we should offer for our daily prayer the very words once used to express the prayers of Christ for Himself. When, therefore, the disciples asked for a pattern that they might pray just like Christ, the spirit of this the opening sentence in His reply was—" No, your prayers are not to be just like mine. I pray after that manner. After *this* manner pray ye. I pray as the *Lord;* but when *ye* pray, say,"—and then He gave them these words.

II. You will also take notice that this pattern was granted after the petition—"Teach us to pray *as John also taught his disciples.* The speaker, and those for whom he was the spokesman, had, no doubt, been in the school of John before they had come into that of Jesus. Yet you are ready to wonder how they could have thought of him just then. They had just overheard that sacred secret, a secret prayer of Jesus. They were still thrilling in the sound of it. You say each one ought to have felt his whole being tenfold alive and awake in that moment of glory and exaltation, and you think there ought then to have been no room for the memory of anything mortal. Yet that prayer at once reminded them of their old master, and their first wish was that Jesus would use John's method of teaching them to pray. He must have been a tremendous man to leave an impression on the minds of his scholars that was keen even in the sharpness of such an excitement. Surely we cannot yet have realised what he was, or what power he had for a time, on the men of his day. After a night of four hundred years, up sprang this flaming morning star. The nation was startled by a holy novelty. When all the romance seemed to have faded out of its life, and all its religion had sunk into common place, John was like one of the old prophets alive again. We must not suppose that he only rang the monotone, "Repent, for the kingdom of heaven is at hand!" In this phrase is given only a summary of his sermons. Though we have no preserved memorabilia of his teaching, it is certain that there was great variety in it. Passages written by the evangelists, show that Pharisees and Sadducees, publicans, soldiers, and persons of every class, went to him with questions of conscience, and had his counsel. No notes survive of the instructions he gave to his disciples, but there can be no doubt that some of these were precious as the gold of heaven, and naturally some of the most precious would be on the subject of prayer. Perhaps no man then living knew more about this than did he. "Filled with the Holy Ghost" from his childhood, he had lived in the wilderness in all weathers. When the wind sang dismally along the river, when the sun struck down with silencing blow, then was he alone with God, inspired with the thoughts that God speaks only to the seeker who dares to be thus alone. He was specially a man of prayer, and prayer must have been one of his special subjects as a teacher. He had secrets to tell about it, and methods to prescribe which his disciples would think matchless. We cannot by any means agree with those expositors, who imagine that he was like the Rabbis, who each gave to the students of his own school some particular form of prayer for daily repetition. The glory of John as a teacher would most likely be, that imitating no Rabbi, and using no conventional plan, he would teach prayer in a way that was all his own. He might have given his pupils a pattern, but would not have taught by pattern only. At the same time it is probable that the request, "Lord, teach us to pray, as John also taught his disciples," had reference in the first instance to the grant of such a form. ·Anyway, there was much imperfection in it. The disciples had no right to speak to their Lord in anything like the tone of dictation. While they asked Him to teach them, they told Him how to do it, and indicated the kind of teaching they preferred. They named the best model. They seemed, as they pointed to John, to say, there—we want you to give us a form like one of his! But Jesus passed by the fault, recognized the necessity, and was pleased to formulate a prayer for the help of their weakness, and also of our own; for on us also His eye rested as He gave it, and all who are trying after closer fellowship with God, may now feel their way, think their way, and pray their way through these great words.

III. Take note of the fact that this pattern *was given twice*. Christ had already given it once, that is, in the sermon on the mount. These suppliants, as if they had never heard of it, asked Him to give what He had already given. How was this? We suppose that, besides the disciples who came from John to Jesus at the commencement of his ministry, and the story of whose call is told in the opening of the fourth Gospel, there were others whose enrolment came later, and that some of these having been with John during the first delivery of the Lord's prayer, made the appeal which led to this, the second delivery.

Strange that they should have been content to miss so much! Why did they stay with John after he had pointed out Jesus to be the Saviour? and how could they stop looking at the finger post instead of travelling in the road? Perhaps they considered themselves, so to speak, to be all the time, scholars in Christ's school, though in John's class, and as spiritual infants, still needing his elementary lessons; perhaps they understood that they were bound to wait with him who said, "The kingdom of heaven is at hand," until that kingdom had come; perhaps there were times when he wavered, making them waver; perhaps as his fame fell away, and his strength broke down, the spirit of chivalry kept them at his side; perhaps he was a man, who under his roughness had, as rough men sometimes have, a loving gentleness that held them with more than magnetic charm. But one day there was a feast in the castle, perhaps on the very floor under which the prophet was imprisoned, when, all at once, amidst flowers fragrances, and shooting rays of gold and silver amidst the clink of drinking cups, and the crash of pitiless laughter, a dead head was placed on the table in a charger. Whose head? John's disciples knew. It was the head of their dearest, their most revered; of the man who had said, "Behold the Lamb of God!" and who had taught them how to pray. They took the body, buried it, then "went and told Jesus." Did they not stay with him from that time, and would they not say, "Lord, to whom shall we go but unto Thee? thou hast the words of eternal life"? But they had come late to school! They had more to learn than their class-mates. They had missed the sermon on the mount. Their new companions, spiritually dull and slow, had not told them that the Lord had already given a pattern of prayer, they therefore asked for one, and the compassionate Saviour gave them the substance of his former words. This was only like Himself, the Teacher who has infinite patience with our dulness, stoops to us, repeats His lesson, and is for ever saying, "Learn of Me, for I am meek and lowly in heart."

IV. Let me now remind you that this pattern of prayer must always *be taken in connection with, and be explained by, the whole of the Christian revelation.* If you are in the stir and current of modern thought, spoken or printed, you will often hear one man say "I want none of your theology, give me the sermon on the Mount;" and another, "I want none of your creeds, the Lord's prayer is enough for me;" and another, "Jesus Himself taught, not a creed, but a prayer." There is a spirit of intolerance abroad usurping the name of liberality. Persons will tolerate Christ on the Mount, who will not tolerate Christ on the Cross; they will tolerate Him as giving the Lord's prayer, but will not tolerate Him as the living way for its acceptable presentation; they will tolerate all who think as they do, distinguishing them as "broad," while those who differ, they brand as "narrow." It is common for disciples in this school to take the sermon on the Mount, including this prayer, as containing the perfect fulness and finality of Christ's teaching, and because they think it does so, they have at least a dormant belief that all other parts of the Bible are comparatively inferior if not needless. At the same time, they regard these words as so wonderfully plain and easy as not to need

GIVEN AS A PATTERN. 39

explanation. "Is it not an odd thing," writes one whose genius gives his words great influence, "that the common fishermen and boatmen by the Lake of Galilee, understood the message that Christ taught them just at once? and now-a-days, when we have millions of churches built, and millions of money spent, and tons upon tons of sermons being written every year, we seem only to get further and further into confusion and chaos. Fancy the great army of able-bodied men that go on expounding and expounding, and the learning, time, and trouble they bestow on their work, and scarcely two of them agreed, whilst the people who listen to them are all in a fog. Simon Peter and Andrew, the sons of Zebedee, must have been men of extraordinary intellect. They understood at once, and were commissioned to preach." We quote this as a fair summary of opinions now afloat with respect to theology and the Lord's prayer, but we venture to say that certain mistakes run through these opinions.

It is a mistake to take this, or any other sectional part of revelation, as if it were the whole. All words spoken by Christ, whether by His own lips directly, or by men whose lips His fire had touched, are of equal authority. The New Testament is *one* Book. It is now present with us totally, is offered to us at once, is all before us at the same time, one part as well as another. Take one, take all. We are to read this part of the book in connection with the other parts, carefully, constructively, putting two and two together, and trying to see how all the parts fit into one development.

It is a mistake to treat this as Christ's final disclosure of grace. That was given gradually. The sermon on the Mount, including this model of prayer, was at an early stage of it, and His earlier words are to be explained by His later. It was not His way to anticipate. The time had not come for Him to "speak of His sufferings" as man's way to God. The discourse to which this prayer belongs is a description, not of the Gospel, but of the kingdom to which the Gospel is the gate.

It is a mistake to say that this part of the Scriptures is so plain as not to need exposition. The multitude did not understand it, or they would not have insisted on its Teacher being crucified. His disciples did not understand it until the facts of the Gospel were accomplished and the spirit was given. With astonishing dulness they constantly missed their Lord's meaning, and when He gave them this prayer, so far from seeing what it meant, it seems to have slipped from their memory, and they at least said nothing about it to the new recruits.

When, therefore, anyone says, "the sermon on the Mount is gospel enough for me, the

Lord's prayer is silent about the doctrines of the Trinity, the Atonement, justification by faith, and the regenerating Spirit," we might answer, "Who gave the Lord's prayer?—the Lord," the Lord who has been crucified, and who offered on the cross the sacrifice by which forgiveness is possible; who has said, "I am the Way;" who is our "righteousness;" "who ever liveth to make intercession for us;" who has told us that we "must be born again;" and has given us "the Holy Spirit of Promise." All the prayer is in harmony with these doctrines, and must be taken in connection with them. Speak of which you will, the Gospel or the Lord's prayer, the one is woven into the text, and is essential to the completeness of the other.

V. It is a pattern meant for the use of *all* the children of God, whatever their differences in age, capacity, or attainment. Some of them belong to one tribe, some to another; some are very young, some very old; some have been learning for half a century, some have only entered school to-day; yet this is for them all. "Not for all," some object. So far from thinking with those who regard it as a lesson in prayer, so very easy that it is too simple to be simplified, we have met with some on the other hand, who regard it as too profound for the use of any but pilgrims of great experience. "It is so deep," we have heard an old Christian say, "that I never teach it to a child." As this exposition is for a *Household Library*, pardon a simple household story.

Dr Jonas King once went into an orphan school for infants, stepped on to the platform, and beckoned the children to stand around him.

"So this is an orphan school?" said he. "I suppose that if I were to ask you, you little scholars would tell me that you have no father or mother."

Some shrill voices said, "Yes."

"How many of you have no father? Answer by holding up your hands."

There was a forest of little hands held up.

"So you have no father?"

The children said they had not.

"Now say the Lord's Prayer?"

They began, "Our Father who art in heaven—"

"Stop, stop!" said the doctor, "is that right?"

They began again—" Our Father—"

"Stop again," he said. "Did you say, Our Father? Yes, you are right, you have a Father. I want to speak to you about Him."

Then, when their attention was awake, he told the story of their heavenly Father's love. The Lord's Prayer was not quite a mystery to the congregation of infants.

As we look into this well, we look through words of wonderful clearness down into a wonderful depth. The oldest saint has not sounded it, yet it is so simple that even a child can understand enough of its real meaning to make it his own real prayer. It names the whole world's wants, yet that little one can use it. It fits the child, it fits the man, it fits the father and mother, it fits the youngest saint, and the saint with reverend head—

> "On which from opening gates have shone,
> The glories of the great white throne."

If Christ had left for our pathway of praying language, words of passion, or utterances of sublime expression, true only in moments of rare light or exaltation, that sometimes would not have been true prayer for us, for it would not have fitted our average life, but this always fits us. It fits every mood and stage of our soul's history—it fits us when our wants are few, when our pulsations are quiet, when our thoughts are level; it fits us when we are just beginning and when we are just ending our journey. So, when I am but a very young child of the Most High, the moments of weakness will be rare indeed when I cannot speak this language, and be stronger for it, but if I have just come down from the third heavens, feeling that henceforth I shall *be* more than I ever yet have been, all the life of my soul rides out in these words, and by this expression, that life gets to be more strong, rapid and victorious. The prayer is, to borrow the beautiful words of Augustine, "little to the little and great to the great. Each word is a seed, and the growing power of the praying life we put into it, gradually makes it throw off the husk and become a tree." Christ has taught doctrines in human words which may be understood more or less by every mind, each mind having its own separate power of understanding them. All the while, does still deeper truth lie hid in his language, waiting to be growingly discovered by growing grace—the more grace, the more knowledge. As it may be said of Chemistry and Botany, of the arts and sciences, of music and beauty—their laws do not stop where our minds lose them; so it may be said of the truths here. From infancy to age, it helps everyone who has in him the life of God, to fresh visions of his glory, fresh discoveries of his meaning, and no part of his Word should make us more ready to say with Luther—"I adore the Divine fulness of Scripture."

VI. This pattern is intended to *furnish certain rules and methods of prayer*. Some of these we may be allowed to make notes of, abstaining from enlargement.

Petitioners are here taught *brevity*. A classic biographer says of one who made a great show in his day, yet had but a shallow soul, that "he could speak much, and yet say little." Some prayers seem to be after this standard. Writing to the Lady Proba, Augustine reminds her that "much speaking is quite a different thing from much praying."

It must be understood that this has no reference to secret prayer. Such prayer is seldom too long. Perhaps it would be well for some of us, if sometimes we rose in the night, or contrived to break away from occupations in the day, so as without the sense of hurry to wait upon the Lord "in praying silence or speech." Indeed in our united as well as in our individual histories there may be special times calling for special continuance in supplication. But when, from much work or much weakness, we are short of time or scant of breath, it inspirits us with new vigour to read how the Supreme Teacher, after telling his pupils that they will not be heard for their much speaking, gave them this scheme of devotional words as if from example of "the much in little."

They are taught to shun *vain repetition*. Perhaps the term "battology" which is thus translated in our English New Testament, does not merely refer to the repetition of words, but also to their senseless multiplication,* repeating the same prayer in our devotional appeal is not

* Matt. vi. 7. The charge μὴ βαττολογησητε is explained by πολυλογία "much speaking."

always a vain thing, for Christ Has sanctioned it by his own example. The real meaning of the charge seems to be "babble not." It has often been said that "battology," the word used by the Evangelist as the nearest Greek equivalent for the Syriac word used by our Lord, came into circulation and grew into force from Battus, the name of a hymnist known proverbially in his day for saying the same syllables over and over again in his addresses to the gods. Whether so or not, the habit was not peculiar to him, but has been the mark of heathenism all time through, and all the world over. We have one sample in the prayer of the priests who cried from morning even until noon, saying, "O Baal, hear us!"* We have another in the Ephesian mob, shouting for two hours, the liturgical phrase, "great is Diana of the Ephesians!"† Instances have been quoted from poets to show how the fashion belonged to all ancient idolatry. Indian monks, we are told, echo for days to-

* 1 King xviii. 26. † Acts xix. 34.

Gilbert Wakefield in his New Translation of the Gospel by Matthew (1782), quotes in illustration: Terence Heautont, v. 880. "Ohe! jam desine deos, uxor, gratulando obtundere .... illos tuo ex ingenio judicas, ut nihil credas intelligere, nisi idem dictum est centies. Pray thee, wife, cease from stunning the gods with thanksgiving. .... unless thou judgest them by thyself that they cannot understand a thing unless the same thing is repeated a hundred times."

gether, the sacred syllable *Um.* Hindoos repeat the name of *Ram* over and over thousands of times. Mahomedan dervishes keep on repeating the word for God, going round in circles while they say it, until they faint. Some phrases are repeated thirty times in a single Mahomedan prayer.* A more remarkable thing however, is the way in which professing Christians vainly repeat the very prayer given by their Master as an antidote to vain repetitions. † No section or class of Christians can claim freedom from the sin ; not one can venture to "cast the first stone," and say, look at us, we never utter needless or thoughtless words in our speech to God—but all need this hint from heaven.

They are taught to pray using these very words. The second announcement of the pattern was prefaced by the phrase " when ye pray, say," the language following. But mark the proviso. It implies that when we do *not* pray we may *not* say it. The point is, that we may only say it when we *do* pray. Prayer is a distinct thing from the vehicle of prayer. Beautiful as this

* " Land and Book," 26.

† See Tholuck on Matt. vi. 7. He says 'according to the Rosary, the Paternoster (Patriloquia, as it was called) is prayed fifteen times, and the Ave Maria 150 times.' We have in a Psalter addressed to Jesus the word Jesu repeated fifteen times together, with only " have mercy on us, help us," intervening. Beza has said " Battologiæ pontificæ vel Satanum ipsum pudent."

frame is, it is only a vehicle of praying life, not a substitute for it. It is no rigid and iron enclosure holding prayers that are ready made for us; it is no petrified prayer, waiting outside our living selves; it is no mere lesson that we may learn with diligence and repeat with senseless accuracy, as birds learn to speak; it is no written Paternoster for priests or saints to touch and bless; it is no verbal spell to conjure with; but it is a divine formula which we may use daily to our unspeakable advantage, and while it is a model, it is also a mould through which we may pour out our new, living, flaming supplications.

It is a *social* prayer. "Souls are not saved in bundles, the Spirit saith to the man, how is it with thee—*thee* personally?"* So, in teaching us to pray, Jesus begins with the individual. After He has said to each apart, "*Thou*, when thou prayest enter into thy closet, and when thou hast shut to thy door, pray to thy Father, which is in secret;"† He goes on to say "after this manner pray *ye*," then when each child has been with the Father alone, he comes out into the family circle and joins with the other children in this praying concert.

They are taught to pray "*after this manner.*" Such is His own phrase, used in giving this edict of grace for the first time. "After this

* Emerson. † Matthew vi. 6.

manner," as to our devotional temper, "after this manner" as to the things to be sought for, however we may expatiate or particularize in the language of our request, everything we need, comes under the head of one or other of these seven summaries or breviates. "After this manner," as to the order of our petitions; so that we may give to each petition its right place in the scale of urgency, and its right subordination to, or power over, the other petitions in the train. There is touching pathos in the plaint of Job:—"O that I knew where I might find Him! I would order my cause before Him, and fill my mouth with arguments!"* Important as he felt it to have right arguments, he felt it to be also important that they should be presented in right order. By the framework of devotion here raised for us, Christ teaches us this right order, showing not only what we should ask for, but what we should ask for first, what next, and on to the end. If in the mere mechanism of our prayers, we may not always choose this progressive sequence, we must, at least, keep this pattern before us as a general guide to their spirit and structure. "It is a regulator by which all ages should set their devotions." †

* Our *pater noster* is apt to begin at *panem nostram*. Anthony Faringdon, Works, iv. p. 262, 1829.
† Hannah More's "Sketches," &c., 1819, p. 472.

VII.—It is right to call this pattern *the Lord's Prayer*. This title has been strongly disputed, but we still stand up for it, regarding the question as one not only of verbal accuracy, but of practical importance.

Some would prefer to call it *the Rabbis' prayer*. They tell us that Jesus is not the author of it, but that He only caught up certain Rabbinical phrases current in His day, and wrought them up into this composition. If so, it would be impossible for them to prove it, for no written collection of Rabbinical sayings was commenced until nearly two centuries later; but what if they could prove it? Say that the Rabbis gave some of their sayings to the Lord. Who first gave them to the Rabbis? The Lord. "Truth," saith St Ambrose, "by whomsoever uttered, is of the Holy Ghost."* It is possible, indeed, that at the time of the Incarnation, forms of petition were used by certain devout "masters in Israel" with which the sentiments of some petitions in the Lord's prayer are in harmony, for, "with the Law and the Prophets," why should not gracious souls express themselves graciously?"† In that case, however, they were only original with Him Who in all ages is the Teacher of prayer.

* "Veritas, a quocunque dicator, a spiritu sancto est."
† Note on Lord's Prayer in Geikie's "Life of Christ." 619.

The Lord's Prayer was not culled from Pharisaic rosaries, and was not merely made up of pearls picked from the dust-heaps of the Talmud.*

Others would prefer to call it the *Disciples' Prayer*. They say, "It is not the Lord's Prayer, but the Disciples' Prayer, for only the disciples are to offer it. We might as well say of the Remembrance Feast, it is not the Lord's Supper, but the Disciples' Supper, for only the disciples are to keep it. In the one case as in the other, the common denomination is plainly the correct one; for the social use of this prayer and the social celebration of the supper, are alike the Lord's appointment. To say, "our tongues are our own, who is Lord over us? We are our own judges of what we should say in prayer, we see no necessity for what has been urged and we disallow dictation," is to run a great risk: we must be careful lest we not only slight a privilege but break a law. The Lord had spoken. The disciples said, "Lord, teach us to pray," then, accepting the title, and exercising the authority of Lordship, He gave

* In all commentaries now within reach of everybody, quotations are made from Lightfoot, Wetstein, Scottgen, and others, of passages collected from Jewish sources, said to have parallel in the Lord's Prayer. One need only look at them to see that our Lord's teaching was altogether independent of anything that the Jews had already taught themselves.

this. As the Lord's Supper is a remembrance feast, this is a remembrance prayer, always to be in our ears, always before our eyes, to show what we should pray for, and how we should pray; until at "our Father's loved abode, our souls arrive in peace."

III.

THE INVOCATION.

"Our Father which art in heaven."—LUKE xi. 2; "Our Father which art in heaven."—MATT. vi. 9. *Authorized Version*.

"Father."—LUKE xi. 2. *Revised Version*.

THIS passage is in two parts, and for the sake of greater clearness we shall think of the two successively.

I. "OUR FATHER."

In the revised version the reading of the text in Matthew is that of the ordinary translation, but the reading in Luke is only "Father." This, however, when interpreted by the connection, comes to the same thing, for if we, with all the other children, speaking to the same Hearer of prayer, say "Father!" of course we mean *our* Father.

I. From the title "Our Father," applied to God, all who bow to the teaching of Jesus infer at least, and before anything else, that God is *a Person*. "It is the tendency of many minds to regard the Deity as a principle rather than as a person." * When this doctrine rules, it puts prayer out of the question, for who could pray to a principle, appeal to the abstract idea of friendship, supplicate the law of gravitation, or intercede with the unknown essence of infinite space? While the world is full of sunshine, and life is a dream of enchantment, you may not care about the subject, one way or the other; but when you have to pass through sharp tests, stern changes and black storms, the want of a watching, speaking, looking, listening God, will be felt as an infinite want. A leader of thought in Germany, famous as a poet, famous as a man of letters—who had through his long literary career fought against the idea of a personal God,—when poor in purse, paralytic in body, and in his last week of life, wrote thus to one of his old class-mates, and under its style of banter I detect a pathetic minor of earnest feeling.

"A religious re-action has set in upon me for some time. God knows whether the morphine or the poultices have anything to do with it. It *is* so. I believe in a personal God. To this we come when we are sick to death and broken down. Do not make a crime of it. If the German people accept the personal King of

* Chalmers's "Natural Theology."

Prussia in their need, why should not I accept a personal God? My friend, here is a great truth. When health is used up, money used up, and sound human senses used up, Christianity begins."

There is an atheism abroad that has in its language a tincture of almost pious devotion. Some of our neighbours are trying to divorce Christianity from Christ, and to have a religion for their God instead of having a God for their religion. Theorists there are, who call themselves Christians, and who profess their belief in the usefulness of prayer, who yet, when asked if they believe that God is a person, will answer —"Not exactly." Perhaps they confuse the idea of personality with certain other ideas perfectly distinct from it. The word suggests to them the idea of a life shut up within the boundaries of form, or in some other ways limited like the life of human beings—who are the only *persons* they know; and perhaps simply from what they mean to be reverence for the Great God, they are unable to regard Him as a Person. Yet they will tell you in confidence that they would feel uneasy to begin the day without the prayer which they had been accustomed to repeat from childhood. What is the use of praying to that, which, not being a person, cannot hear or speak? Extremes meet. The savage who prays to a stone, meets on the same level with this man of refinement. We say, in the words of the mystic—

> "To own a God who does not speak to men,
> Is first to own, and then disown again ;
> Of all idolatry the total sum
> Is having gods that are both deaf and dumb."*

Jesus, the teacher of prayer, has given us the first rule, "when ye pray, say Our Father." His first doctrine therefore is, that God is a Person. You never say Father to a force; Father to a law; Father to a mist; Father to a mile, nor to infinite millions of miles in a line; "Father" is not the name for Thought apart from the Thinker, nor for Friendship apart from the Friend; nor for a Link, though the first link in a long chain of grand phenomena. If we mean more than a figurative father, we mean by that word a living Person. In our world, sure as a son is a person, a father is a person; and Fatherhood implies personality in God, truly as it does in man.

II. The title "Our Father" belongs to God as *the Father of all mankind*. What is said now, and what will be said in the next section, make two halves of one complete statement, and must be taken, not separately, but together. I say now, Man; whoever you are, and even though you are now under a sentence that deprives you of every family title, the glorious

Dr John Byrom.

Person of whom we have been speaking is your own Father. He is so in this sense: all human life began in Him. Although He has given us our bodies transmissively, He has given us our souls immediately; it is the doctrine of our philosophy as well as of our faith, that, while He is the Framer of our bodies, He is the "Father of our spirits," and that each man of you received his soul direct from God as the first man did. Glimpses of this truth seem to have been caught in the twilight of ancient Heathenism. Ages before the Gospel sunrise, a poet had spoken of the supreme Spirit as "Father of gods and men." The name *Jupiter* was compounded of Deus and Pater; and the like sentiment was breathed in a certain Greek verse* quoted by Paul in his oration to the men of Athens, and which was at the same time turned by him into an argument against idolatry. "As certain even of your own poets have said 'for we also are his offspring.' Forasmuch as *we* are the offspring of God"—we thinkers, we reasoners, we sculptors, whose magic almost makes the marble breathe,—we who have wills of our own, we who have love, conscience, and all the powers of personality, "*we* ought not to think the Godhead"—that is, to think that *our Father* "is like unto gold, or

* Sir Walter Raleigh gives several instances of this kind in his "History of the World." Book . section 2.

silver, or stone, graven by art and man's device" *
The argument is, "*as* certain of your poets
have said," so it is, God *is* your Father; then,
appealing to the principle "like father, like son,"
he blames them for paying the honour due
only to their Father to that which is no relation
to them whatever, but altogether of another
and an inferior nature. In doing so he takes
this old sentence from their literature, stamps
it, gives it currency as a divine saying, and it is
now a doctrine welded into the sacred text,
that even idolators are "the offspring of God."

It is true that "all have sinned and come
short of the glory of God." It is true that
while men are "alienated from the life of God,"
God is nothing to them, as the most tremendous
reality in the living world is nothing to the
dead. And it is true that no one while in that
state, or on the strength of the creative tie, has
a right to a child's place or a child's inheritance
yet it is also true that God is the Author of all
human being,—this, once a fact, is always a
fact. Speaking to all men, however wide their
wandering, or deep their fall, we are permitted
to say, Although sin has destroyed the filial
spirit in you, and made you by your own act,
outcasts from the presence of God, the change
is not in Him, but in you. He is to you, not a
foe, not a stranger, not a taskmaster, not even a

* Acts xvii. 28, 29.

king, first of all,—but a Father. In Him is an infinite store of unappropriated love, and of power waiting to be trusted. Why are you so slow to believe in this glorious reality? When your children go wrong, do you fathers cease to be fathers? Do you not care? Have they become nothing to you?

A rumour once reached Andrew Fuller that his wild son Robert, who had been impressed as a sailor on board a man-of-war, had been tried for desertion, and had died under the infliction of a stern sentence.* The father's words about this, have condensed into them all the agony of grieved affection, and seem like bitter drops of distilled pain :

"In former cases my sorrow found vent in tears; but now I can seldom weep. A kind of morbid heart-sickness preys upon me from day to day. Every object around me reminds me of him! Ah! . . . He was wicked, and mine eye was not over him to prevent it; . . . . He was detected and tried, and condemned; and I knew it not; . . . He cried under his agonies, but I heard him not; . . . He expired without an eye to pity or a hand to help him! . . . O Absalom my son! my son! would God I had died for thee, my son!"

Does any father think this the language of extravagance? Did not this father feel so much

* This rumour was afterwards proved to be false.

for this wanderer, just because he was a wise and good man? Is there less concern on account of rebellious sons in the heart of the wise and good God? and is human paternity more tender than the divine? Is there no pity in the cry "Hear O heavens, and give ear O earth; . . . for I have nourished and brought up children, and they have rebelled against me?" Hear how he vindicates his parental character: "How shall I give thee up, Ephraim? How shall I deliver thee, Israel? How shall I make thee as Admah? How shall I set thee as Zeboim? mine heart is turned within Me; my repentings are kindled together; I will not execute the fierceness of mine anger, I will not destroy Ephraim; for I am God and not man":— not less than man, but infinitely more.

We endorse the sentiments on the Fatherhood of God expressed by Luther. He was one day catechising some country people in a village in Saxony. When one of the men had repeated these words, "I believe in God the Father Almighty," Luther asked him what was the meaning of "Almighty"? The countryman honestly replied "I do not know;" "Nor do I know," said the catechist, "nor do all the learned men in the world know; however, you may safely believe that God is your Father, and that He is both able and willing to save and protect yourself and all your neighbours." "Almighty God is the lovely Father of mankind."

THE INVOCATION.

III. God is "our Father," *through Jesus Christ.* We proceed to this statement, on the principle already noted, that this pattern of prayer must always be taken in connection with, and as explained by, the whole of the Christian revelation of which it forms a part. This revelation as given by Christ in person began in His discourse to Nicodemus. Speaking to "the master in Israel" in the dialect of ceremonies which he was supposed to understand professionally, and as a matter of course—Jesus said, "Except a man be born of water and of the Spirit, he cannot enter into the kingdom of God," "ye must be born again." There is, so it seems to us, a plain reference to the prophecy of Ezekiel.[*] "Then will I sprinkle clean water upon you and ye shall be clean." . . . "a new heart also will I give you, and a new spirit will I put within you:"[†] The water spoken of, being that which was familiar to the Jewish worshipper water stained by the blood of sacrifice, and called "clean" in a ceremonial sense, because in that sense it made clean the man on whom it was sprinkled. The fulfilment of the type shewn in the "water" is therefore now to be found in "the blood of Jesus Christ . . . . which cleanseth from all sin." Reading the whole of what Christ said to this enquirer, we see that

[*] John iii. 5, 6, 7. [†] Ezekiel xxxvi. 25, 26.

the Spirit is the agent of regeneration, that "the precious blood" is the instrument of it, that faith on man's part is the medium for receiving it, and that the first act of that faith is identical in time with the first moment of the "life everlasting,"* "For God so loved the world, that he gave his only begotten Son, that whosoever believeth in him should not perish, but have everlasting life." So does He "devise means that his banished be not expelled from Him."† When, for every purpose of communion, sin has dissolved the original tie of sonship, thus does He answer His own question to the sinner, "How shall I put thee among the children?"‡ God was in Christ, therefore, in giving *Him* He gave *Himself*. His rebel children would not believe that He loved them. They always thought that He had to be placated by some terrible sacrifice of their own. Jesus came to show that they had quite misunderstood the Father, and that the Father by the gift of His own Self in His own Son, would *give* the atonement which they had supposed Him to *demand*. In the moment when we begin vitally to know this, and to trust ourselves to it, we begin in reality to live, for in that moment the new and everlasting life is born. True, God is already our Father, and while we are still in rebellion He so

* John iii. 16. † 2 Sam. xiv. 14.
‡ Jeremiah iii. 19.

loves us as to offer us the "Unspeakable Gift," but if we refuse it, this Fatherhood may not lawfully keep us from perishing. The Fatherhood that saves, begins not with the first creation, but with the second; not when we are born, but when we are born again. So Christ teaches us in His first discourse on Salvation, and in His last, we hear Him say, "I am the way, and the truth, and the life, no man cometh to the Father but by me."*

Besides his own direct instructions, we have the following and similar words written by his inspired scribes: "He came unto his own, and his own received him not. But as many as received him, to them gave he power to become the sons of God, even to them that believe on his name; which were born, not of blood, nor of the will of the flesh, nor of the will of man, but of God." † "Whosoever believeth that Jesus is the Christ, is born of God." ‡ "*If* any man be in Christ, he is a new creature; old things are passed away; behold, all things are become new." § "Ye are all the children of God by faith in Christ Jesus." ¶ "And because ye are sons, God hath sent forth the Spirit of his Son into your hearts, crying, 'Abba, Father.'" ‖

Then, after all, some will say, your doctrine

---

* John xiv. 6.　　† John i. 11, 12, 13.
‡ 1 John v. 1.　　§ Cor. v. 17.
¶ Gal. iii. 26.　　‖ Gal. iv 6.

of the Divine Fatherhood comes practically to this,—that He is only the Father of a few Christians. According to you, millions of the human race who have the natural right to say "Our Father," are no better for that right, because they know nothing of Christ who is the only way to the Father. This is not what I say. The most of what I venture to say may be cast into the form of two suppositions:— Suppose on the one hand the case of a man brought up with a Christian education and living in a Christian atmosphere, holding in his hand or having within his reach, the whole gospel revelation; suppose that man shall make a small selection from it and fling away the rest—suppose that he will not accept the doctrine of sacrifice, will not own himself beholden to Jesus Christ for salvation,—suppose him to say, I scorn theology, I repudiate mediation, I will go on my own responsibility straight into the presence of God, and shall deem it enough to repeat this beautiful Lord's Prayer— would that prayer be accepted? Not, certainly, if the words just cited, which reveal the way of a sinner's access to God, are true—and true they must be, for they are the words of God. Indeed, if prayer is to be regarded as an act of faith, this would not be a prayer at all, for it would not be an expression of faith. No man can be said to have faith in God who has not faith in all

God's plain words. If the gospel be true, to utter even the Lord's Prayer without acceptance of the gospel is to defy the law of God and to refuse His love.

On the other hand, take the case of some poor waif of humanity, young or old, in our land or in any other, who had never even heard the name of Jesus, knowing nothing, but feeling much; sorry for sin, yearning for love, suppose him just to say out of his heart these two words—"Our Father," having heard them spoken somewhere—I should say that such a prayer was prompted by the unknown Holy Spirit and accepted through the unknown Jesus. I am reminded of the man healed by Jesus, of whom it is said, "he that was healed wist not that it was Jesus." There would be, I think, in that poor suppliant's heart, and ready to spring from his lips, the question—"Who is the Lord, that I might believe?" Though he does not know him yet, he will know him soon. The dawn has begun that will shine "more and more unto the perfect day."

I do not know the secret history of our ignorant prayers in their movement in the mediatorial counsels of God. I do not know how far the efficacy of the dying intercession extends—"Father, forgive them, they know not what they do!" I do not know, definitely, but I indulge the happy thought that through

Jesus, when there has been no opportunity for Him to be heard of, many a prayer like a rocket of distress shot up from the wild sea and the dark night, has brought help from the heavenly Father. It is gloriously true that the Fatherhood in the thought of which Christians rejoice, is the correlative of that sonship which we receive when we believe. For all that, I would say do not wait to utter this prayer until you are sure that you are regenerate. Let any one of the race, conscious or unconscious of regeneracy, cry out these words from the depths of his life, then that fact will be a proof that Jesus is teaching him to pray, and a prophecy that his prayer will be heard.

IV. In teaching us to say "*Our* Father," Jesus would remind us of our *Brotherhood*. Common prayer to the common Father, suggests a common interest, and helps to keep it alive. Sin separates. The sinner is an egotist. The motto of the world is, "Every man for himself." An isolating principle is at work in every one who has turned his back on the Father, the result of which is seen when, in the language of the world's own shrewd vernacular, his one thought is for "number one." This is mirrored in the parable of the prodigal. When the younger son left the *Father*, he wished to divide his interests from those of his *brother;* and his demand was—"give *me* the portion of goods that falleth to *me;* but when he came back, his greatest joy was to be received as one of the family. The individual child is not indeed merged in the family; but though each one may and must pray for himself, and say "*my* Father, give *me* my daily bread, forgive *me*, lead *me;* at the same time, every one whose heart beats with the new life, will not only sing a new song, but breathe a new prayer—this prayer, that rises in concert with all the family and that opens with the cry, Our Father!"

First and chiefly are we reminded by it of *the fellowship that knits together Gods elect.* On the evening before his death, Dr Chalmers, while walking in his garden, was overheard to say in earnest, low tones, "O my Father, my heavenly Father!" When I can say that, then any man in the world who can also say it, is my brother. "Dost thou see a soul that has the image of God in him? Love him, love him! This man and I must go to heaven some day. Love one another, do good to one another." This charge to all the holy brethren spoken by John Bunyan in his last sermon, has lost none of its point by change of circumstances, none of its sacredness by lapse of time; I must not, however, insist on seeing in a soul all that special family likeness which Bunyan calls the image of God, before I give that soul my love, nor must I mistake for love what is only a

romantic tenderness for the distant or the dead—
for the distant, whom I suppose to show, for
the dead whom I suppose to have shown, this
likeness, more than it is shown by Christians
living near me now. Christians living now, and
with whom I have now to do, may sorely try
my loving power; but so, if brought into
actual contact with them, would those have
done whom I exalt as my ideals. Much of the
charm that good men of other lands or times
may have for me, may be but the charm of that
"distance which lends enchantment to the view;"
or the magic tinting of a visionary picture;
contact with their very counterparts living in
my own land and time might shatter my dreamy
preconceptions, and make my radiant fancies
fade. Let me be sure of this and act on it; if
I, and the man at whom I am now looking,
are both in Christ, he and I are brothers, and
"brothers evermore." Whatever may be the
drawback, whatever the weakness, whatever
even the vulgarity on the surface—there is the
family life below—sense under the nonsense,
soul under the body, truth under all the mistakes; within the earthern pitcher the fire;
behind the rough shell the pearl; beneath the
ragged thistles and stinging nettles of the field,
the treasure; and concealed for the present by
much that may excite the scorn of the foolish
and the pity of the wise, that which will shine

out gloriously in the day of "the manifestation of the Sons of God." Not only am I one with that man, but one with all the multitudes who hold "like precious faith."

> "Our teachers taught that one and one make two.
> Later, Love rules that one and one are one."

Later still, the love of God works a greater wonder, for grace turns millions into one. "We who are many, are one body in death." The waves are many, the sea is one; the boughs are many, the vine is one; the stones are many, the temple is one; the children are many, the family is one; and as one family, we say, "Our Father!"

While "in spirit and in truth" we pour out our prayers in these divine, delightful words, we pray down blessings not on ourselves restrictively, but on the church at large. If we believe in the real power of prayer, we must believe that this prayer which we offer as a family, has real power to bless us as a family. I gain good from it as offered by my brothers and sisters; they gain good from it as offered by me. In some sense, sometimes traceless, but always true, multitudes whom I have never heard of, and who have never heard of me, are the better for it. Ordained by God, it has an instrumental value and a mystic potency in fetching down daily supplies, daily applications of forgiving love, daily shelters from temptation and daily deliverances from evil in which all the children share. "There is a certain spiritual traffic of piety betwixt all God's children, wherein they exchange prayers with each other. Am I weak in spirit and faint in my supplication? I have no less share in the holiest suppliants than in my own: while there is life in their devotions, I cannot go unblessed." Such is Bishop Hall's commentary. And Leighton, with the like spirit says, "Every believer hath a share in the prayers of all the rest, he is a partner in every ship of that kind that goes out to sea, and hath a portion in all their gainful voyages."

Besides the good from it shared by all Christians, there is a further benefit. "Our," is *a word of love that takes in all men*, for, "have we not all one Father? Hath not one God created us"? Those who offer it with more or less consciousness, in the name and grace of Christ pray for and try to pray with all men. As belonging to the human race they pray that the good things here named may be given to the human race, where they are wanted. In the spirit of the prophet, when he said "unto us a child is born, unto us a Son is given," in the spirit of the Apostle who, speaking to an angry crowd, said, "Men and *brethren*," the disciple who makes this his prayer honours all men, carries out the rule "add in your love of the brethren, love,*—

* Malachi ii. 10.   2 Peter i. 7—*Revised Version.*

love to those outside the church, love after the pattern of the great love wherewith God loved us, even when we were dead in sins."

II.

We now come to the second section of the verse—" which art in heaven."

There is a relation between the word "heaven" and the word "heave." We have these words from our Saxon fathers, who were not given to think ideally, and who, pointing up to that life or state of life which they thought of as lifted or *heaved* by the Creator to the utmost possible glory and bliss, called it "heaven." * This word gives the essence of the meaning conveyed by the Greek original, which seems to have been derived from a root signifying "to rouse, or stir up," and which therefore suggests height, or elevation.† Physical altitude has always been used as the type of what is the purest, noblest, and best; we speak of high standards, high principles, and high aims; in this way, we find that all through the Bible, the word "heaven" represents the idea of loftiness, and the two phrases, "high as heaven," "deep as hell" express the two extremes of height and depth. While we confess our inability to unfold the import or to grasp the strength of the word heaven, it seems

* *On heofonum.* † 'Ορω.

to us that it is used here mainly to remind us how high in excellence God is above earthly fathers. The relation He sustains to us is too comprehensive and too intimate to be perfectly represented by any earthly tie, but that in which it finds its nearest equivalent, and from which he takes His favourite name is "Father;" but the fatherhood is that of the "high and lofty One," and Father "in heaven" means "Father in perfection."

1. Perfection of *love*. We can only learn heavenly things from earthly types. Looking at such types, what is your idea of what a Father should be? At least you understand that the word represents *love*—love that thinks, love that works; the love of one who is wise, who is strong, and who takes trouble. It means this in man, it means this in God, and to perfection. Does not a natural father take pleasure in his child? How is it in your own knowledge and experience? Is not that pleasure in your heart one of the most pure and tender that you know? Is it less so in the heart of the heavenly Father? That which makes a father gentle to infant weakness, that which makes him, though "master of sentences," listen with delight to his child's first stammering speech, that which cheers the young life in all its blundering steps upward, that which makes a father pleased when the child gets on well at school, pleased to see

his own likeness come out in the child's face; that which makes him live in his loved one's honour, ready to die in his shame; that which makes him feel no gladness like that in his son's promotion; that which gazing on the clawed, stained, and trampled garment brought for him to look at, says, "It is my son's coat; an evil beast hath devoured him, . . . I will go down into the grave unto my son mourning;" that which, after all, makes him willing rather that some "evil beast" *had* devoured him than that he should live to forsake his principles or cloud his stainless fame; that which makes a father "take pleasure in infirmities" and self-denial, in working days and sleepless nights, and in whatever may enable him to lay up for his child,— a pleasure which delights to be trusted and which hungers for love — all that — has its existence from, and its highest perfection in, Him who is our Father in the Highest.

We know it now. But there was a time when each one who now is a Christian, was ignorant of it. Perhaps his heart said to God "Oh Thou great Iron"!*

There was once a son who left his father's house, and went to "a far country," that he might live in glorious independence. Divine influences moved in his heart one day, and a

* So began a threatening letter to Prince Bismark, Berlin, July 29, 1881.

new spirit started into life. He was like an outcast saying to himself:—

> "Does that lamp still burn in my father's house
> Which he kindled the night I went away?
> I tarried once beneath the cedar boughs,
> And marked it gleam with a golden ray;
> Did he think to light me home some day?" *

"Then he arose and came to his father." How he, though the vilest sinner, sorry for his sin, was received, is told in the well-known tale which is a prophecy as well as a parable. That loving picture of a father, who, in the gaunt, weary, haggard, tattered tramp, while yet "a great way off," sees his long lost child, rushes out to meet him, clasps him to his heart, wraps round the rags of his disgrace the folds of his own garment, weeps over his neck the tears of enraptured affection, calls for the best robe, and has struck up for him the music of the instant festival,—represents the mighty love of our Father to us on the day, when through the secret impulsion of His grace, our ragged, starved souls, weary of sinning, weary of repenting, weary of self— came home to Him; and since that day, we have been making ceaseless discoveries of that love; we have been going on to verify the fulfilment of the parable, and to understand the mysteries of the ring, the robe, the sandals, the feast, and the music of God Himself, as He

* Christina Rossetti.

THE INVOCATION. 75

"compasses us about with songs of deliverance."

Perfection of *help*. "If ye then, being evil, know how to give good gifts unto your children, how much more shall your Father that is in heaven give good things to them that ask him?" * That word "if" seems meant not only to imply an argument, but to suggest a question. "*If* ye . . . know how!" Do fathers and mothers always know? Look at Hagar, when the bread was gone, the water spent, and Ishmael ready to die of want, did *she* know? "She cast the child under one of the shrubs"—and "she went and sat down a good way off, as it were a bow-shot; for she said—Let me not see the death of the child. And she sat over against him, and lifted up her voice and wept." Look at certain times, into certain houses not far from your own, and you might hear a child ask for bread, and then hear the father say "there is none." He would help but he does not know how. When the tiny frame is racked with agony; when the white little face turns on the pillow, when the lips quiver with rapid breath, and no words come, when the eye of pitiful entreaty looks into the father's very soul, and seems to say "cannot *you* help me?" what can he do? He does not "know how to give the good things" needful, and in blind sorrow

Matthew vii. 11.

bursts out of the room. It is natural for the father to be the helper of the child. The *super*-natural is not the *contra*-natural : it is only nature heightened to a degree above anything that we can understand. God, as our helper, because he is our Father in heaven, might say to us "as the heavens are high above the earth, so "—in helping you, "are my ways higher than your ways, and my thoughts than your thoughts." *

Perfection of *nearness and observation*. Joseph would have been saved from the rage of his brethren in the day when they sold him into slavery if his father had been looking on. It was well for the little Shunamite when under the blow of the sun-stroke that his father was near, so that he could say to him " my head, my head." But the earthly father cannot be always with his child : the heavenly Father can be. Men are slow to understand this. When they say the words "Our Father which art in heaven ";—they seem to feel that " heaven " is a fact in their astronomy rather than a doctrine of their faith ; and they have the drifting fancy, if not the distinctly outlined thought, that their Father lives in one world, and they in another. " Do not I fill heaven and earth," saith the Lord. " Heaven is my throne, earth is my footstool." He who is in His nature so exalted, that heaven

Isaiah lv. 9.

THE INVOCATION. 77

being His throne, He rules the universe, must fill the universe. As God, His nature is without limitation. When Jesus was dropping the garment of our limited nature, and was about to ascend into the glory which He had for our sakes laid aside for a time, He said to Mary, "Touch Me not, for I am not yet ascended;" that is, "touch Me not while I am on earth, wait till I am in heaven, then touch Me."

The Jesus whom men once saw was farther off than the Jesus of whom we say "whom not having seen, we love." Wanting His help the sisters of dying Lazarus despatched a messenger: we need only despatch a cry. The messenger brought Him in four days; a cry brings Him directly. Are you in some sore strait? Quick, quick, let your heart run, your feet need not. Cry to the Father, and God will come to you in Christ. We speak of the rate at which light travels, or electricity, or sound; but who shall say how short the time prayer takes in reaching the ear of the Father, and gaining the reply! "It shall come to pass, that before they call, I will answer, and while they are yet speaking I will hear." *

Ages ago, a man was telling his companions the story of how he had been nearly shipwrecked within sight of land. At one moment the ship was riding over the crest of a mighty wave, when

Isaiah lxv. 24.

there was a glimpse of the pier crowded with people,—the next moment it would be like a thing groaning and hissing in the trough of the sea. Some of the passengers wildly prayed to the virgin mother, some to St James, some to St Christopher and some to other saints in glory. His friend said, "to whom prayed you?" His answer in substance was, "What could Dominic, or Thomas, or Catherine do for me? thought I, St Peter is nearer to the throne than they, and if I pray even to him, I shall be drowned before he has time to plead my cause. I must needs go straight to Him who made me, and the sea, and the saints, so I went straight to my Father myself, saying 'Our Father which art in heaven, save these poor souls and me that now cry to Thee for bare life!' Not one of the saints can hear more quickly than He, or grant more freely what is asked." *

Perfection of *homeliness*. Let no one take exception to this word. The grandest being in the universe is the homeliest, the Being of all beings least to be afraid of, and to whom the frightened child who knows Him runs for comfort. We have no perfect sense of rest in God, until we have along with our adoration, this feeling of homely rest, for we are so made, that He

* This is the idea given in the dialogue entitled "Naufragium;" a long passage in the "Colloquies of Erasmus."

is our heart's dwelling-place, and we are restless until we rest in Him. Pity the mortal who sees nothing in the universe more than awful order, dread magnificence, and the working of cold material laws.

Times there will be, in the history of a man without God in the world, when he will feel like a child who has wandered into a factory, is lost amidst the machinery, is at once fascinated and empowered by its heavy, invariable motion— motion without a soul in it—who feels that he cannot get out of the way of its grind, and "dare not let his shriek go free." One who had held the creed of atheism, afterwards told his friends that when at length he was able to believe that a God was really alive, he " danced with delight," although he had not then reached the experience of hope in Christ. "It is a blessed thing," cried he, " that we are not placed amid the grinding and wheeling of a great Machine of a universe without guiding hand or animating heart. There is a God! there is a God! Jehovah, he is the God! Jehovah, he is the God "* He got to believe in God yet more grandly and tenderly, and no disciple was ever led more than he into the secret of rest that comes from saying to the God of the universe, " Our Father which art in heaven." The child yearns to be at home with the Great Spirit; amidst the vast-

* Dr John Duncan.

ness and glory of the scenery around him he cries for his Father; longs for his loving ear, his familiar voice, and the shelter to which he may nestle with a sense of friendliness, security and peace. This unspeakable want is met when we find the Father, whom the Teacher of prayer reveals.

The words—"Our Father which art in heaven," suggest to us *the perfection of our home*. Although the word "heaven" is here used mainly to remind us of our Father's perfection, it is meant also to remind us of the family home. Some Christians seem not to care for this doctrine, and in giving us their own views they are almost as refined as Confucius, who said. "Heaven is Principle." Our notion, although it includes this idea, does not stop at it. It includes not only character but condition, not only principle but place. We look upon heaven as the perfect home of perfect human nature, Human nature has a body as well as a soul, and the body asks for place. These expectations chime with and are cheered on by the words of our Teacher. "In my Father's house are many mansions: if it were not so, I would have told you, I go to prepare a place for you; and if I go and prepare a place for you, I will come again, and receive you into myself; that where I am, ye may be also." *

* John xiv. 2, 3.

THE INVOCATION.

We distinguish between presence and manifestation. We think of God as a Spirit who is present in all places at all times; yet we think of heaven as the one place of his highest personal manifestation through Jesus, "the Lamb in the midst of the throne." There, and thus, God is at home! In this, as in other things, the earthly must furnish us with the types of the heavenly. A man's house is the centre of all that he lives for, and all that he does. It is the place which he will be sure to fit up and adorn in a way equal to his resources and worthy of his station. There the man of rank, the man of wealth, the man of refined taste or various information, will have his appropriate surroundings; and there, where he is at home, his children will be. What must that place be in which even God is at home! We cannot tell, and it is astonishing that any mortal has ever tried to tell. It is written in an old story that an artist, led by Indians, once went to paint Niagara; but that when he saw it, he dashed his disappointing pencil down the precipice, for he felt that he could as soon paint the *roar*, as the fall, the foam, the great sheets of light, the arch of coloured rays, with all the other wonders that went to make up the surprising cataract; and shall we who have only seen earth, try to picture heaven! No! poems of glory, pictures of magnificence, all fail, "imagination in its utmost stretch, in wonder dies away;" in our present state, our future state is a mystery, though a mystery of delight. It is our home, but the celestial homeliness is beyond us now. The "gates" *may* be "ajar," but they are not wide open; only a blinding ray shoots through from the light within. We see that there is a glory, but not what the glory *is*. Not only because we are so sinful, but because we are so human, the idea sometimes seems to us as appalling as it is glorious, alarm almost overpowers delight; and we understand the confession of a saint who said, "If I saw a door opened in heaven," I should be afraid, and cry "O Lord not to-day!" Yet no child need fear. The heavenly condition will be natural, as soon as we are born into it, and sure as we are now born into grace, we shall one day be born into glory. The heavenly antitypes of sky and water, trees and flowers—things of nature and art, will be to us there what these things are to us here. Human dearness will wax, not wane; God will make it all perfectly right, familiar and delightful, and each timid Christian must now learn to say, "then shall I be satisfied when I wake in Thy likeness!"

While we are like children at school, or out on the travels that belong to our education, it is good for us that there should be this reference to heaven wrought into the very texture of the pattern prayer, and connected with the very name of our Father. The thought of heaven thus mingling with our prayer is to have a power over all the life. Heavenliness is to influence our earthly pleasures, earthly sorrows, earthly cares, and earthly business. "So," says Chrysostom, "withdrawing him that prays from earth, and fastening him to the place on high and the mansions above."

IV.

THE FIRST PETITION.

"Hallowed be Thy name."—MATT. vi. 9. LUKE xi. 2.
Authorized and Revised Versions.

I. What do we mean by the Name of the Father?

II. How can we "hallow" it?

I. What is meant by the phrase, "my name"? The learner might say, you have been speaking of "our Father," *who is he?* To answer this question would be to give you His name. A name is now only a mark to distinguish one person from another; but originally it was not only indicative but expressive. We still keep to this old meaning when speaking of God's name. His name is the expression of Him, or the discovery of Him, written out or spoken out, in this, that, or the other language. We know that one language differs from another language in glory; that some languages are not made to carry so much meaning as others; that the language of savages is mainly adapted to express the meanings that belong to the life of the senses, and that the language of educated persons is adapted in addition to express the life of the soul. In illustration of this, we may quote a remark once made by John Henry Newman—"It is of no use trying to translate the ideas of Plato into the words of the Hottentot." So, as to the languages that God speaks or writes. He reveals His name through them all, but all are not adapted to convey those highest and latest revelations which we are dying to know.

1. His name is the expression of Himself through the language of *Nature*. With more or less distinctness of inscription and splendour of enchantment His perfections express themselves there, and there those living letters start forth by which we spell out His name. In the smallest as well as in the greatest things, we see some revelation of the Infinite. We all know what a little desert flower said to Mungo Park, whose eyes were perhaps the first and last to see it. There, blooming alone in what looked like a wilderness of sifted ashes, the little thing caught his eye, and just as he was at the point of despair, whispered in his ear the name of his Father, so rousing him to noble enterprise. The Name is revealed everywhere to those who have eyes to see and ears to hear. Go out in the sunny wind of spring, look on the awakening loveliness, listen to the enchanting commo-

tion of Nature's harmonies, and you must learn something of the Name. Go out into the harvest field, and it shines in burning glory. Look up into the sky through showers, and certain words of Mr Ruskin may come to mind—" All these passings to and fro of fruitful shower and grateful shade, and all those visions of silver palaces built about the horizon, and noises of moaning winds and threatening thunders, and glories of coloured robe and cloven ray, are but to deepen in your hearts the acceptance and distinctness and dearness of the simple words, 'Our Father, which art in heaven.'" Look out into the white, wavering snow; if, yesterday, you had caught up one of the million million snowflakes then falling, that you might look for your Father's name even in that, you would have found it. What a wonderful wealth of beauty was in the crystal flowers of tender whiteness, melting the moment you put them under the microscope, yet not before you had caught a vanishing glimpse of what you wanted to see. Look on the winter landscape, you see it; on the winter water, you see it; for God expresses Himself on the water as much when the frost has shot its tracery over it, as when in the spring it reflects the fringing flowers. Look up into the heavens that declare His glory in the night; then look down on the glory that shines reflected in silver glance and gliding wave, that makes magical sights in misty distance, and that spreads itself in broad imperial sheets of light, revealing hints of the unfathomable name.

Yes, but Nature's language, wonderful as it is, is not rich enough to speak out all that I need to learn. There is much after all to be learnt about Him before I can feel safe or happy. To say the least, I find that changes, working death as well as life, are always going on in Nature. Mornings are not always clear and cloudless, the lark is not always pouring out its morning hymns, the dews are not always on the grass like dazzling drops of light, nor is the river always a rippling splendour. Blights, infestations, and east winds make desolating changes in what was bright with hope and beautiful with promise. Do these changes express the name of God? Is He kind to-day, cool to-morrow? Does He take me up to-day, drop me to-morrow? Sometimes for me, sometimes against me? Nature has no answer. I meet with greater perplexities still, when passing through the deeper experiences of life. . If in my distress I study Nature by the help of such books as the "Bridgewater Treatises," designed to shew "the Power, Wisdom, and Goodness of God as manifested in the Creation," still I am confounded. God is kind to the innumerable living things in air or water, and has wonderfully fitted them each for happiness in its own element. But God is very kind to the shark as well as to the life which the shark snaps at. The African tourist riding through the wilderness pauses to notice the gazelle waft with airy grace down to the lip of the river—stop, shiver lightly, then stoop to drink. He may say, "you thing of beauty, you express a thought of Him who is the Infinite Beauty!" While he says so, he is magnetically conscious of another presence,—turns in his saddle to look, and in a moment feels as if lifted and lighted, for what is that? He sees silently, swiftly trailing through the leaves, straight to that "beauty," a bristling lion, with eyes like electric lights, with a bound and a spring, and a roar that shakes the air—down with smashing blow, the lion drops on to the gentle creature at the stream. God made the lion. He is very kind to him. "The young lions roar after their prey, and seek their meat from God." So in human life the inequalities, the mysteries of pain, the sufferings from heredity, the long years of injustice that once made a poet cry, "Right is for ever in the dungeon, Wrong is for ever on the throne;" and the vast spaces of the earth where the people, as it seems to us, for no special fault of their own, "sit in darkness and the shadow of death;" all these things seem to cloud over the glory of the Father. Much may be learnt of Him from the kingdom of Nature

and the chapters of Providence, but not enough
for the like of me, a sinner. After all that is
told, so much remains untold, that I am sometimes in a storm of consternation. I try to be
righteous, but it is poor work. Looking at the
name of the Lord only as revealed here, I am not
able to say, "the name of the Lord is a strong
tower, the righteous runneth into it, and are safe;"
and I am not inspired with confidence to sing,
"The glories that compose Thy name, are all
engaged to make me blest." No, when I feel
fit for nothing, there is no comfort for me in
the doctrine of the "survival of the fittest"—the
doctrine which seems to be written on the
pages of Nature; when I am sinking in weakness,
it is no comfort to me to hear from Nature, the
only gospel Nature preaches, the Gospel of
"salvation to the strong." When my heart is
breaking because I have to say, "Lover and
friend are put far from me, and my acquaintance
hast thou hid in darkness;" there is no comfort
for me in the things that naturalists discover,
however great or educated my interest may be
in such discoveries. There is no whisper of
rest from the wave, or of pardon from the breeze,
or of immortality from the sunshine! Nature is
to me a realm of riddles. Providence shows
me the universe, "not in plan, but in section."
I am not able to form a judgment of the temple
from a stone, nor of infinite machinery from

the wheels that move just in sight of me. God refuses to let us see all that He is; to use a blunt phrase, but with reverence, "I cannot make Him out!" and my heart cries, "O Thou great, beautiful Mystery, tell me, I pray Thee, Thy Name!"

A recent sage whose decisions are still accepted by many as those of an oracle, having on one occasion spoken of the first Epistle to the Corinthians as being part of a Bible about the divine authority of which many wise and good men have been doubtful, went on to say, "at anyrate we are sure that in the rocks, and seas, and stars we have the authentic handwriting of the Most High."* Yes, but we are equally sure that since the rocks, and seas, and stars were made, the family calamity and disgrace has come to pass that with terrible brevity we call the fall; for common sense tells us that the Holy, Wise, and Happy God is not the Fountain out of which sprang the unholy, unwise, unhappy life of men as men now are. There must have been a change since the first. It is small comfort to know that we have in the creation "the authentic handwriting of the Creator;" for what He wrote *before* the fall tells us nothing to meet the case that comes *after* it. I hear that there is another will, and indeed there must be, for the arrangements made for unfallen creatures

Carlyle.

could not fit the fallen. I want the last news from heaven; a fresh message from the throne, telling us what is to be done *now*, and how the new dilemma must be met.

2. His name includes the further expression of Himself through the medium of inspired *words*. "The last news from heaven," "the fresh message from the throne" made needful by the changed condition of things, we have in the words of the Bible. Thus we have an advance not only in the matter of revelation but in the mode of it. Words are more distinct and exact instruments of expression than are things. Thoughts, reasons, definitions can only be sharply outlined and vividly tinted by words; therefore, while some reasoners are asking the question with a smile at the comedy of the idea, " is it likely, now, that the eternal Spirit should reveal Himself to man by a book-revelation?" I am thinking that it is just what might have been expected, and that in so doing He acted like Himself. He who at the fitting time always uses the best means in order to the best ends, has done so in this instance, and when the case required it, poured out the glories of His name through words—words of prophecy or history, words of gracious talk, or stately oration, or pungent proverb, or thrilling verse, spoken or written by holy men of old who were the consecrated organs of divine expression. Some

powerful disclosures of Himself were gradually given in those various titles which we call His names. Read some of them. Jehovah, the "I am," the Everliving One, who is, and who was, and who is to come; El Shaddai, the Almighty; Jehovah-jirah, the Lord providing a ransom; Jehovah-rophi, the Lord our Healer; Jehovah-nissi, the Lord under whose banner our souls win victory; Jehovah Sabaoth, the Lord of the hosts of heaven whom idolators worship, the Lord of the hosts of Israel,—the title one day to be merged in the famous title of Christ, "Head of the Church; Jehovah-Zidkenu, the Lord our righteousness; Jehovah-Shalom, the Lord Peace; Jehovah-Shamma, "the Lord is there," making the glory of the mystical Jerusalem. These and other appellatives, usually called names of God, were in fact different revelations, helping to disclose the one great Name. In the earlier dispensations, to those who trusted Him, God was all that these words stand for. The time had not come for them to know why, for the saving grace which these and other words revealed, existed on account of a certain basic principle, or central arrangement, as yet out of sight, and which was to be explained in "the fulness of time." While we have only the Old Testament in our hands, still we wait, there is more to come than this; beautiful and inspiriting as they were, most of the revelations by words were founded on, and were prophetic of a greater revelation still to be made.

3. His name is perfectly expressed to me in the language of *the Incarnation*. "To whom will ye liken God?" not to a man, surely! Yes, to a man. But "His thoughts are not as our thoughts, neither are His ways as our ways." "No, the sea is not as the standing pool by the road side. Yet, when the breeze crisps the pool, you may see the image of the breakers and the likeness of the foam. Nay, in some sort, the same foam. If the sea is for ever invisible to you, something you may learn of it from the pool. Nothing, assuredly, any otherwise."* The great enquirers of antiquity had reached the truth that a perfect human person is the most perfect conceivable form of a personal revelation—that we can have no clearer notion of a perfect person than through a perfect man. They looked round for one, and when he was not to be found, genius tried to give the ideal of him in statuary. If a Greek had said to his priest, show me God the Father, he would have taken him to a temple, would have lifted a veil, and pointing to a certain colossal image wrought by Phidias, would have said, "there, *there* he is!" Never before on this earth had been sculptured a form into which had been

* Ruskin.

struck such towering majesty, or a face into which had been flung such soul. Mailed in gold of the morning, girdled with gems of rarest water, when the sun shone on it, it shone back a second sun; and it was verily thought that the Deity had come down to inhabit that miracle of man's device. Yet, the poor trembler, looking at that sculptured man, would have said in his heart, "No, no, that will never do, that is not 'the brightness of the Father's glory, the express image of His person;' that is not the exponent of God; if it be so—hard as His jewelled coronet, cold as His marble throne, high above all passion or compassion, there is no sympathy to be looked for from a God like that. A flash from that eye I can understand, but not a tear in it; his very whisper would deafen me, if he were to speak I should die."

Christians as we are, we bow to an image, and God himself has given it. The use of an image in worship is a sin only when it breaks the law, "thou shall not make to *thyself* a graven image to bow down to it and to worship it." It is the obedience of faith when the soul has for its resting-place of thought and help to prayer that living image which is furnished in the divine plan of redemption. "God is only knowable through the medium of humanity," and the humanity set apart for this, is that of the perfect man, Jesus Christ, "the man who shall be as a hiding-place from the wind and a covert from the tempest, as a voice of water in a dry place, and the shadow of a great rock in a weary land;" the man "who is the image of the invisible God, the firstborn of every creature: for by Him were all things created, that are in heaven, and that are in earth, visible and invisible, whether they be thrones, or dominions, or principalities, or powers; all things were created by Him, and for Him; and He is before all things, and by Him all things consist."* "Lord, show us the Father," said Philip. "Jesus saith unto him, Have I been so long time with you, and yet hast thou not known Me, Philip? he that hath seen Me hath seen the Father, and how sayest thou then, Shew us the Father?" Would you know the love of the Father? look at Jesus; to know his holiness? look at Jesus, to know how He feels toward mankind. Do you wonder how men dare to love a Perfection so grand and high? look at Jesus. Do you find in an ancient declaration of His name that He "will by no means clear the guilty," and do you wonder, therefore, how He can save sinners? look at Jesus on the cross. Jesus is our theology. Jesus is the Word—all words in one, and through Him, God is no longer the Great Anonymous. He explains Creation; He explains the Old

Col. i. 15, 16, 17.

Testament. When in the last stage of His journey to the cross, the dark shadow of it fell upon His spirit, He said, "Now is my soul troubled, and what shall I say? Father, save Me from this hour: but for this cause came I unto this hour. Father, glorify Thy name!"* and at the close of His high priestly prayer, spoken just before he stepped down into Gethsemane, He said to the Father, with reference to His disciples, "I have declared unto them Thy name, and will declare it." Jesus is the revelation of God, and the New Testament is the revelation of Jesus.

II. What do we mean by praying that the name of our Father may be hallowed? In the language of the Old Testament, to hallow a thing was to set it apart ceremonially, as a thing specially august and sacred. The temple enclosure was hallowed ground, because it was set apart from all other ground, as the one spot sacred to the ministrations of the priesthood. The vessels of the temple were hallowed because they were so set apart for sacred purposes, that their use for common purposes would have been profanation. The word used in the Lord's prayer is meant to convey the same idea.†

* John xii. 27, 28.

† Perhaps the word Ἁγιασθητω is from a negative, and and γη, the earth. It answers to the Hebrew הַקְדִישׁ and קִדֵּשׁ. This meant first, to make holy an unholy thing;

"What is this?" asks Augustine, "can God be holier than He is?" Not so, but our conception of Him may be holier than it is. We pray that He who is separated only by His perfections from all other beings, may be so regarded ; and that more and more, in our own souls as well as in the souls of all men,—in our thoughts, motives, desires, and actions, also in theirs, He may be thus venerated and glorified.

2. "Hallowed be Thy name," by *the indwelling of the Holy Ghost* in us. We shall not even see the name so as to hallow it, until the divine enlightener creates the seeing spirit. When Peter, in the flash of an amazing moment, read God's name in Jesus, it was said to him, "Blessed art thou Simon Bar-jona, for flesh and blood hath not revealed it unto thee, but My Father which is in heaven."* As it was in him, so it is in us. We must say of the things of Christ, "Eye hath not seen" them, "but God hath revealed them to us by His Spirit." "The heart," says Pascal, "has reasons which the reason does not understand," and by the Spirit in the heart making the heart see things which

---

next, it came to mean to treat a holy thing as holy, that is to honour it as such. Ex. xx. 8 ; Lev. xxi. 8 ; Num. xx. 12 ; Deut. xxxii. 51. In these passages, to sanctify or hallow, means to set apart in a venerating way from earth, and all mere earthly purposes.

* Matt. xvi. 17.

confound the intellect, He inclines us to understand Christ, and to trust Christ—brings us into intimacy with Him, and this intimacy works a likeness,—"Beholding as in a glass the glory of the Lord, we are changed into the same image from glory to glory, even as by the Spirit of the Lord;" so, the beginning of all that hallows the name of the Father in us, is the life of the Holy Spirit.

2. "Hallowed be Thy name" by our *trust*. This is our joint prayer, yet let each one in offering it, distinctly pray for himself as well as for others. Looking to Jesus, who is the Father's name alive—alive in one personal, perfect, final revelation, I would say, there, my soul's trust is all there—there alone, as on that which is gloriously separated from and exalted above "every name that is named, not only in this world, but in the world that is to come;" there only, there for everything, there for ever. As "God manifest," as a Being all by Himself, I separate this Saviour in my own mind from all other Saviours. "He hangeth the earth upon nothing;" let my faith like the earth be hung upon nothing but God; by human will as well as by divine ordination, by me, by others, by more and more, may He be set apart as the one foundation of hope, the one life, the one strength, the one righteousness, the one manifested Perfection!

3. "Hallowed be Thy name" in the *spirit of our prayers*. A graphic writer has pictured to us the story of an African journeying to offer his petition when in trouble, to a certain wizard or *Obe* man — his only ideal of Him who hears prayer. He and his companions on their way to the secret place where this "hearer of prayer" had his sanctum, travelled for miles through the wilderness. Spurred on by fear they plunged into the shadowy forest; in the darkness, now and then they were caught in swinging loops of the bush ropes, or were tripped up by treacherous vines, or tangled among the trunks of tree-ferns, or tumbled over vast nests of ants. On, on, they pushed through the dull, green light. They reached at length a spot where the ground was so damp, the foliage so dense, and the atmosphere so faint that it seemed like poison. They had to brave stinging leaf, teasing insect, and deadly snake—when it seemed impossible to get through the tight and netted undergrowth another inch, then, dropping down on hands and knees, they glided silently after their guide through a scarcely discernible opening in the bush, when the man who had the consultation to make, now went on alone. As he crawled, he suddenly touched with naked knee, a large, cold, smooth object, which snatched itself away, and shot back a hiss that thrilled him through. As he still pushed

on, he could hear the noise and sway of snakes, disturbed by his entrance; he crept, and crept on, till at last he found himself entered upon a wide, cleared space of considerable size, shut in with splendid vegetation around and above. Against the majestic pillar of a central tree, midst mixed bamboos and tree ferns, surrounded by the dense wood, like the very house of death, was the home of the strange Negro. At the sight of him, he began to creep back again, but he no sooner did so, than on all sides there arose a commotion of swarming snakes, that slipped and rustled out of his way.[*] This may serve as a parable. It shows how some persons think of prayer. They have in their hearts some echo of the ancient cry, "O that I knew where I might find Him! that I might come even to His seat! I would order my cause before Him, I would fill my mouth with arguments," but they think of the way to God as a long and difficult journey. They suffer from a sense of hard work, of having to travel over desperate ground, of going through an effort of conscience, making fatigue. The thought of God is always a weight upon their spirits, and there are times when it is a cold horror. They must pray, but, more or less, they are sorry for it, and sometimes it costs them agonies. Making it a terrifying process, they turn it into a violation

[*] From "Lutchmee and Dilloo;" much abridged.

THE FIRST PETITION.   101

of reverence and a mode of profanity. This is not the prayer of one who knows Christ, and who has been born again. Yet it is to be feared that in some instances, at some times, from a stern theology, or through a depressing spiritual atmosphere, even the sons of God pray too much like slaves, and that even by them, the Father, though not *un*known, is *mis*known. Nothing in one who ought to know better, so grieves the Spirit; gives such a wound to the love of God, does such a wrong to His name. His name is Love; let us hallow it. There is no love like His love. To any one who has the faintest faith in Christ, yet who at this moment holds back from the Father, feeling half afraid to take the liberty of prayer, it may be said, "Dost thou think Him 'altogether such an one as thyself?' touchy, jealous, apt to take offence, slow to make allowance, hard to be entreated, difficult to please? Are you thinking of God only as an infinite man—man as man is now? The only man who reveals what He is like, 'is the man Christ Jesus,' and are you afraid of Him?" If your hearts have learnt the words Christ has here taught us, "ye have not received the spirit of bondage again to fear, but ye have received the spirit of adoption, whereby we cry, Abba, Father!" Fear, indeed, you have, but the fear that lifts the soul, not the fear that lowers it. It sends no shudder over the life. Instead of a terror, you feel a glorious awe. By the life of the Holy Spirit within you, live up to your new standard of privilege. Separate thoughts of your Father from thoughts of all imperfect beings, fling off all doubt of welcome, all freezing dread, and with happy freedom, letting yourselves go, run into the all-embracing love.

4. "Hallowed be Thy name" in our *lives*. It is indisputable that it is Christ in us that makes our Christianity. Christians with no Christ in them, are only cheap imitations and hollow shells that infinite Love itself must fling away with infinite impatience. Such lives, more than anything else imaginable, cause the name of God to be blasphemed. The life of Christ in the lives of His people, is that by which it may be most hallowed. "Beloved, let us get holy lives, and leave the rest to God."* Life takes form. The apostle said to the Galatians, "My little children, of whom I am again in travail, until Christ be *formed* in you."† Sure as that life is in us, the form, beginning in the heart, will come out into human sight. What is the form of Christ's life? "He is holy, harmless, undefiled, and separate from sinners." The same life in us, must, in the degree of its existence, take the same form. We are to be

* Fletcher of Madely.
† Gal. iv. 19. *Revised Version.*

separate from sinners, not like the ancient ascetics, who to avoid spiritual infection fled from their presence, and lived in solitary places; but separate while in the midst of them; separate by distinctness of nature; separate, as the salt which though it may be in contact with the earth, is separate from it; and as the light is separate from that which it illuminates. It is said of the glorified ones, who are before God in heaven, " His servants shall serve Him, and they shall see His face, and His name shall be written on their foreheads." The spirit of this petition is, let it be so on earth, so that wherever His servants are, His name may be seen. May His name be in us, and on us, "known and read of all men!" Where we live, there, by the indwelling, formative life of Christ, the Manifestor of the Father's name, may that name be hallowed through our lives! Most hallowed where the most of our lives have to be spent, that is, not in splendid places, but in common places. You have, perhaps, to spend most of your own life amidst things for manufactory, things for cultivation, or things for sale; you are inclined to tell me that there are many small transactions in a sphere like yours, which I 'might call sins, but which are quite necessities as the world now is. Society has such claims, business is so sharp, life is so rapid, competition is so frantically desperate, that if you were, in any sense of the phrase, to hallow God's name in your secular occupations, you would not be able to go on for a twelvemonth. Then you are not able to feel ready for the day when "there shall be upon the bells of horses, 'holiness unto the Lord;'" you are not able to feel that you are always priests,—your working dress priestly raiment; your working place, holy ground,—you are not able to offer the Lord's prayer.

5. " Hallowed be Thy name" in *our language*. Of course, where any temptation exists to the profane use of any word that, like a symbol, stands for God, this is forbidden first of all. It may seem to us quite inconceivable that any Christian should ever thus be tempted, or any persons who frequent Christian assemblies; yet, when a man who has been accustomed in a passion to rap out "bad language" becomes a Christian after his habits of life are settled, there may be a burning moment, when some evil word long unheard on his lips, but all the while sleeping like a memory, a wicked misery, or a motionless torpedo on the floor of the soul's deep sea, may suddenly explode, and rage on the surface, as did the cursing words of Peter when he denied his Lord. In olden times, when the disciples of Christ were new converts from heathenism, and much mire from the "horrible pit," out of which they had

been lifted still clung to them; or in the dark ages when the Bible was a sealed book to the multitude, preachers dwelt almost restrictively on this use of the clause, "hallowed be thy name." Chrysostom, for instance, knew that large numbers in his congregation were profane swearers, and twenty of his homilies against profane swearing still survive.

Bishop Jeremy Taylor, discoursing on this subject, with splendid eloquence and rich mosaic of illustration, speaks thus: "The name of God is so sacred, so mighty, that it rends mountains, it opens the bowels of the deepest rocks, it casts out devils, and makes hell to tremble, and fills all the regions of heaven with joy; the name of God is our strength and confidence, the object of our worshippings, and the security of all our hopes; and when God had given Himself a name, and immured it with dread and reverence, like the garden of Eden with the swords of cherubim, and none durst speak it but he whose lips were hallowed, and that at holy and solemn times, in a most holy and solemn place; I mean the high-priest of the Jews at the solemnities when he entered the sanctuary—then He taught all the world the majesty and veneration of His name; and therefore it was that God made restraints our conceptions and expressions of Him: and, as He was infinitely curious, that, from all the appearances He made to them, they should not depict or engrave any image of Him; so He took care that even the tongue should be restrained, and not be too free in forming images and representments of His name; and therefore, as God drew their eyes from vanity, by putting His name amongst them, He took it off from the tongue and placed it before the eye; for Jehovah was so written on the priest's mitre, that all might see and read, but none speak it but the priest. But besides all this, there is one great thing concerning the name of God, beyond all that can be spoken or imagined else; and that is, that when God the Father was pleased to pour forth all His glories, and imprint them on His holy Son in His exaltation, it was by giving Him His holy name, the Tetragrammaton, or Jehovah made articulate; to signify 'God manifested in the flesh,' and so He wore the character of God, and became the bright image of His person.

"Now all these great things concerning the name of God are infinite reproofs of common and vain swearing by it; God's name is left us here to pray by, to hope in, to be the instrument and conveyance of our worshippings, to be the witness of truth, and the judge of secrets; the end of strife and the avenger of perjury, the discerner of right and the severe exactor of all wrongs; and shall

all this be unhallowed by impudent talking of God without sense, or fear, or notices, or reverence, or observation?"*

It is not the common swearer only, who does that which we thus pray against. It is the sin of prayer-utterers who speak the words of devotion while they are thinking of something else; so making the service a work done by machinery; it is the sin of any speaker or writer who uses the name of God on the vehicle of his own glorification; it is emphatically the sin of those who, perhaps, habitually sit on thrones of judgment, each as an incarnate perfection, and see the children of this world, or the members of the church pass before them with the one idea of determining what sentence they shall pass, but who out of their shallow religiosity, and in their slipshod, random talk, passing for 'religious conversation—sometimes make such free use of the sacred name, that we hear them with a spiritual shiver, and feel a shock almost as great as when a poor ignoramus carelessly let slips a round oath; it is the sin of all flippancy and levity in connection with anything chosen by God as a special medium for the expression of Himself. The Bible, the day of holy rest, the institutions of His grace, are things marked by the King's broad arrow as sacredly His own, therefore, as such, set apart from common uses.

* Sermon on the Good and Evil Tongue.

We must stifle in its first conception, the sense of the comic in connection with the thought of the divine. "Jest not," says Thomas Fuller, "with the two-edged sword of God's word. Dangerous is it to wit-wanton it with the majestie of God; wherefore, if, without intention, and against thy will, by chance medley thou hittest scripture in thy ordinary discourse, yet fly to the city of Refuge, and pray God to forgive thee." We think of all these possibilities of sin, in ourselves or in others, when we cry, " Hallowed be Thy name."

6. "Hallowed be Thy name in the church by the ascription to Thee alone, of the honours due to Thee." One day during the course of recent disturbances in Ireland, an Irish Bishop, giving the people in his discourse a direction on the subject of secret societies, said, "We have received this direction from our Holy Father." Our *Holy Father!* what is his name? We are told that his name is "Leo the Thirteenth." There must be a mistake here. This is not the person meant by Jesus Christ, when He said, "Holy Father, keep through Thine own name those whom Thou hast given Me, that they may be one, as we are."* The devout and loving common sense of Christianity recoils from the application to a man of the title Christ gives to "the High and Lofty One." It is not as if it

* John xvii. 11.

were simply used as the language of venerating courtesy; it is used as the language of religion. It is not so much the title itself that we now think of, as the doctrine it stands for, and which is at the root of the system represented by him who means it. God's title is taken by the sovereign Pontiff, on the theory that he is God's Word and representative. It only means this. Some years ago, in answer to an address read by an English deputation, the Pope said, "I alone, despite my unworthiness, am the true successor of the Apostles, the Vicar of Jesus Christ on earth; I alone have the commission to steer and guide the bark of Saint Peter; I alone am the Way, the Truth, and the Life; all who are with me are with the Church; all who are not with me are without the Church; without the Way, without the Truth, and without the Life. Let all men understand this, that they may not be deceived and led astray by fancy Catholics, who teach and desire something very different from that which the Head of the Church teaches and desires." If these serene assumptions are to be accepted as true, of course he who utters them has a right to be called Holy Father. If they are not true, in so calling him, we hallow the wrong name. We know that the words, "I am the Way, the Truth, and the Life," are the clear and final words of Jesus Christ Himself, that

His was the glory seen by the prophet in his rapture, and that to him rose the cry of the seraphim, "Holy, holy, holy." Only the Father whom we see when we see Him, is the Holy Father, and if we are consistent in the utterance of this ascription, we shall only send it up to God as in Christ, "Head over all things to His Church."

7. "Hallowed be Thy name" in *the overthrow of idolatry*. An idol is that which men on their own responsibility set apart as the name or expression of God, and therefore as the proper object of their worship. Millions in the days of antiquity have so regarded their imperial masters. Where religion is another name for fear, and God another name for Force, this was not so much to be wondered at, for nothing so represented to the multitude the idea of awful power as an Eastern king of kings, or a Roman emperor. Yet He was not only worshipped by the uneducated. Valerius Maximus, addressing Tiberius in the preface of his book, said "Other divinities are only in opinion; thy Divinity we see and touch in thee." Antoninus called himself Father Bacchus; Caligula said to Jupiter, "kill me, or I will kill thee;" Domitian signed his decrees, "your Lord and your God." Heliogabalus proclaimed himself "the Lord Sun." In the day when Christ was giving His disciples their model of prayer, men were finding their

ideas of God's names in emperors, in the storied or sculptural expressions of classic mythology, and in the grotesque shapes before which crowds were kneeling in India. In our own day, there are lands full of idols that look like foul, fantastic, scaring dreams of sin and misery struck into stone. Countless fellow subjects of our own are still in such darkness, that when they think of God, they know no better expression of His name then such images can give. In the Bombay Presidency alone, we are told that more then thirty thousand temples are still devoted to objects of worship like these. When we call these things to mind, when we also remember that an idol is not only an object of worship fashioned with the hand, but is also anything that is instead of God to us, or from which our life takes its supreme law; when we try to count the idols now worshipped in London, and feel that they are numberless; when we lift the veil, look into the shadows within our own spirits, and descry idols there, as the penitent Manasseh saw idols in the Holiest place, we wake up to see the meaning and to feel the solemnity of the prayer, "Hallowed be Thy name!"

V.

THE SECOND PETITION.

"Thy kingdom come."—MATTHEW vi. 10. LUKE xi. 2.
Authorized and Revised Versions.

MARTIN LUTHER, writing in the year 1518, remarks, that when the children say, " Hallowed be Thy Name," The Father asks, " How can any honour and name be sanctified among you, seeing that all your hearts and thoughts are inclined to evil, and you are in the captivity of sin, and none can sing My song in a strange land?"

Then the children speak again, thus:—

"O Father, it is true. Help us out of our misery; let Thy kingdom come, that sin may be driven away, and we be made according to Thy pleasure, that Thou alone mayest reign in us, and we be Thy dominion; obeying Thee with all the powers of body and soul."*

These antique sentences help to show the vital connection between the first and second

---

* This is part of a long and interesting quotation made by Dr Saphir at the opening of Lecture VI. on the Lord's Prayer.

petitions. It is not a connection without consequence, like that of pearls in a circlet, or links in a chain; but thought grows out of thought, and prayer out of prayer, like bough out of bough in a stately, flowering tree.

I. The *kingdom*. The phrase, "Thy kingdom," means Thy "reign." In our language we have one word for a kingdom, another for the reign in it; for instance, we make a distinction between the kingdom of Queen Victoria, and her reign in that kingdom. It was lately said in the House of Commons, that in certain parts of Ireland, the Queen does not reign, but the Land League. Then, although the kingdom is hers, the Queen's reign in it is to come. In the original language of the New Testament, one word is used for both meanings—in one place it stands for the territory under kingly rule; in another place, for the kingly rule itself. Here it stands for the kingly rule. Of course, the earth is already the kingdom of God in the first sense of the word. It cannot come *to be* so, for so it already *is*. But other lords have dominion in it. "An impious war has been declared by the subjects on earth against the Sovereign in heaven: there has been a revolt of the heart, of the intellect, of the senses, and of all the faculties. A general insurrection of the human race against the Creator has been organized in this world. The degraded senses have said, 'Let us break His bands asunder and cast away His cords from us;' the fickle and infatuated reason in its turn has said, 'Where is the promise of His coming?' Selfishness and pride have leagued together, and when the Father appeared in His Son, have exclaimed we will not have this man to reign over us." *

This doctrine is often contemptuously denied. You know many persons who would say, "Nonsense! that doctrine of the fall;—of course, man is as God made him." Facts contradict their dogma. The Greek magician in stone did not make the statue as you find it,—stained, shattered, flung down in the nettles; the Gothic builder did not make Chepstone Castle as you find it, a ruin; the workman did not make the king's banner as you find it, torn, trampled, and ground into the mire; so, God did not make man fallen, lost, and a rebel. Do you say, he is made with instincts to ascend? then some malign hand has arrested "the ascensional development," and brought him down to be what you now behold. True, the heart of humanity is part of God's kingdom; but does He reign in it? Pride reigns, self reigns, animalism reigns, death reigns, but the reign of the Father is to come. In the remarks now following, although we may occasionally use

* Vinet.

the word "kingdom," it is with the understanding that we use it in the sense of "reign."

II. *The way this kingdom will come.*

1. It will come by *the mediation of Jesus Christ*. Intimation of this, couched in "dark and cloudy words," was given on the very day when the rebellion broke out. Then it was said to the serpent, "I will put enmity between thee and the woman, and between thy seed and her seed; it shall bruise thy head, and thou shalt bruise his heel." * This promise of Eden was a bud in which the future flower of all revelation lay folded. As time went on, it gradually opened, and the announcement of a Saviour's coming reign was given with growing distinctness. A promise was made to David that a son of his should have universal sovereignty. "He shall have dominion," so declared the oracle, "from sea to sea, and from the river to the ends of the earth. All kings shall fall down before him; all nations shall serve him, and shall call him blessed. In his days shall the righteous flourish, and abundance of peace, so long as the moon endureth." † In a few years it became clear that neither Solomon nor Solomon's son fulfilled this prophecy; but still, while the glory of the Hebrew nation was waning into gloom, and its power was sinking into nothingness,

* Genesis iii. 15.　　† Psalm ii. 7, 8.

the prophecies of the coming King kept glowing on with greater vividness through message after message, until the last prophet made Him the subject of His last message: when, after the silence of four hundred years, the Spirit spoke again, the speech was still about the King, and the burden of John the Baptist's ministry was, "the reign of heaven is at hand, get ready for it." While this herald's voice was sounding, the King came. He had not been long here—in fact, had not yet in a formal way commenced His undertaking, when, all eyes being fastened on Him, all minds exercised on the question what His kingdom would be like, he issued a manifesto, and we have it in the Seven Beatitudes.* The first beatitude is, "Blessed are the poor in spirit, for their's is the kingdom of heaven." "This," says Augustine, "is inclusive of all the beatitudes, for all the beatitudes that follow are the unfolding of this first one." "We have here, the beginning both of the principles and the blessings that make up the kingdom of God."† Let but these principles, with their consequent blessings, have ascendancy, and there, in all its perfection, is the kingdom. This kingdom, or reign, is one. Part is on earth, part is in heaven, part is present, part is to come; this

* Matt. v. 1-12. † Aug. de Serm. Dom. in Monte.

is the bud, that is the flower; when we die, going through the gate of death is not going into the kingdom, but going into its perfection.

Jesus having in the first section of His sermon on the Mount, told His disciples what the kingdom would be like, before He brought that sermon to a close, taught them to say to the Father, with reference to it, "Thy kingdom come." Guided by the instructions contained in that sermon, the cry of our life must be, "Father, let that reign come, when men shall be poor in spirit, so that all the advantages of the reign may be theirs; when they shall mourn so that they may be comforted; when they shall be meek, and so inherit the earth; when they shall hunger and thirst after righteousness, and so be filled; when they shall be pure in heart, and so see God; when they shall be peace-makers, and so be called the children of God. Let that reign come in which shall come that royal truth, that royal kindness, that royal fairness, that royal peace, that exaltation of graces—which, because common, current language is not intense enough to describe, is set forth in the bold hyperbole of this sermon on the Mount! Let that reign come, which will be the beginning of heaven on earth!"

2. It will come through the *instrumentality*

of the cross. By the cross, we mean what was consummated on the cross. God in Christ founds the new reign of grace in that only. The peace that is signed in the palace of the Most High, is peace through "the blood of the cross." War ceases only when this is operative. We take God's word for this, and lay aside man's opinion about it. On the one hand, it is enough for us to know, that in some way, through the perfection of the life, and the mystery of the sacrifice finished there, the rebel may be forgiven, and yet the eternal order not be broken; on the other hand, to know that while the rebel is looking at and trusting in "Christ crucified," enmity melts, a new life of love is inspired, and that, as far as the influence of the cross extends, the reign of God comes.

Christian men sometimes seem as if they only half believe in this. They seem as if, like the Emperor Constantine, they see a glorious cross, and read the celestial inscription under it, "by this conquer," yet, believers as they nominally are, it is not by this, that is, not by the cross alone, that they expect to conquer, but by the fitness of the means they employ in using the cross, and their real hope seems to be, after all, in the *instrument* of the instrument. There was great hope when the emperor, who has just been named, became champion of the Christians, but that hope was disappointed. It is true, his conversion, such as it was, made Christianity an aristocratic thing,—wealth, honour, office were all on its side, and the creed of the monarch became the creed of the people, but influences were thus set working that tended to poison Christianity and to postpone the coming of the kingdom. When an old Saxon king gave up his gods and was baptized, he would bid his riders to do the same, and they would, as a matter of course, obey their master's bidding. Equally as a matter of course, Christianity would become the fashion, but the heathen people though marked with the sign of the cross, were heathen people still,—still trembling in terror of the spiritual world and the hidden wrath of nature. The unknown powers they once worshipped through such old names as Freya, Thor, and Woden, they still worshipped, though under such new names as the Virgin Mary, Saint Giles, or Saint Lawrence; and the kingdom of the Father seemed to be very little nearer than it was before. It is true in modern as in olden time, that when fancy Christianity, or any other version of it, gets married to rank and social status, even the world will join that church, fashion will profess that truth, and infidelity will make believe to believe; but it is not in this way that the kingdom will come. Great things for the Gospel have been expected from education, from traffic, and from the advancement of science, but these are not the primary instruments for bringing about a chosen, cheerful subjection of hearts to the King who is a Spirit and whose name is Love. Sometimes, when a nation professing to live under the standard of the cross, has had brilliant martial successes, and heathen peoples have thus been brought under its sway, this has been gloried in as a fact on the side of the Gospel. The horse "paweth in the valley, and rejoiceth in his strength, he goeth on to meet the armed men. He mocketh at fear, and is not affrighted; neither turneth he back from the sword. The quiver rattleth against him; the glittering spear and the shield. He swalloweth the ground in his fierceness and rage, neither believeth he that it is the sound of the trumpet. He saith among the trumpets, Ha, ha! and he smelleth the battle afar off, the thunder of the captains and the shouting."* It is not in such fields that He who leads "the armies of heaven" rides forth to victory. War may in a single day stop the beat of thousands of hearts, quench the light of thousands of eyes, and make showers of tears fall, but though the Master of all things, good and evil, may use this evil thing for clearing obstacles out from the path of His kingdom, it is not by it that the kingdom will come whose

* Job xxxix. 21-25.

gentle glories are depicted in the sermon on the Mount. The one instrumentality for setting up that kingdom in human hearts is the cross. This alone makes it possible for the Father to welcome the wandered ones who come back to Him, and, at the same time, makes them glad to obey Him as their King. When even by the humblest words or deeds we publish this cross, we are taking part in some degree in working the machinery which the King Himself has appointed, and in the single use of which He will win back His dominion over the human will.

3. It comes *by the power of the Spirit.* Think of an avalanche coming down from above the snow-line of the Alps. See it, it is coming with stern, conquering sway, to carry all before it, but at first, its kingdom "cometh not with observation." It slips along with slow, scarcely perceptible motion. In time, you begin to see it crawl, crawl down the incline. "It is coming!" cry some watchers from the valley below; but they get used to it, give over fearing, and go on with their work or their play. One day, all the people are in terror; it is coming, and they now know it, but what can they do? Set up a barrier? raise an army? plant and point great guns at it? say "stop!" Do what they may, on it comes. It comes faster and yet faster, "darting down the slopes, flitting from shelf to shelf, jarring the mountain where it strikes," still

glancing, shooting, bounding on, starting vast rocks, loosening forests, sweeping away grassy acres along with it as it flys,—with gathering mass it gains gathering mountains, until it thunders over into the vale below and entombs a village.

Whose hand cut that stone from the Alp? who shot it? who flung it into the green gulph? Ah! it was cut without hands, and in our world of forms, forces, and movements, it is the most impressive symbol we know of gathering, rushing power that is not of man.

Once in a vision of the night, the Spirit of Prophecy showed an avalanche to the King of Babylon. He had in the same vision seen "a great image," whose "brightness was excellent," and "the form thereof was terrible." Then "a stone cut from the mountain, without hands," smote the image, which was of iron, clay, brass, silver, gold, and broke all these in pieces. Through the lips of Daniel the prophet, the "Revealer of Secrets" showed that the terrible image, fashioned in different parts, of different materials, represented the great, successive ruling powers in the future of this world. "In the days of these kings," thus said the Lord, "shall the God of heaven set up a kingdom which shall never be destroyed; and the kingdom shall not be left to other people, but it shall break in pieces, and consume all these kingdoms, and it shall stand for ever. Forasmuch as thou sawest that the stone was cut out of the mountain without hands, and that it brake in pieces the iron, the brass, the clay, and the gold ; the great God hath made known to the king what shall come to pass hereafter ; and the dream is certain, and the interpretation thereof, is sure."* So will the kingdom of God come. Man works with his hands, and this kingdom will come as such a stone comes, "without hands." It will come, that is, without that power of motion which begins in man's working, here fitly symbolised by "hands." It will come by the power of its own divine vitality and momentum. It will come in Gospel truth, instinct with the life of the Holy Spirit, reigning in the lives of more and more believers, until "the earth shall be full of the knowledge of the Lord as the waters cover the sea." So mighty and universal shall this reign be. It will come not as a blow scattering terror, not as an avalanche of death, but as that which will only kill evil, and under whose prevalence, "mortality shall be swallowed up of life." Thus shall rise the " Stone of vision, overlooking all the realm of the earth."

III. *How we should pray for this.*

1. Every one of us must pray that the king-

---

* Daniel ii.

dom may *come in his own heart*. The speech of each one must be, though I am the king's child, through "having received the Spirit of adoption;" His reign in my heart is still a process, not a complete result, and in the full sense of the word His kingdom though coming, is not yet come. My prayer ought to be more than it is,—Let thy kingdom come in *me*. It is sadly symptomatic of my soul's ill health that I find myself offering prayers for so many other things before this. I want His forgiveness, I want His comfort, I want His light and protection, I want His support in what I suffer, and His blessing on what I do, but I do not yet feel as I ought to feel, and pray as I ought to pray for the reign of His grace in me. I am sometimes ready to say, Father, save me out of my afflictions, let me come home; let this wicked Absalom, my soul, see the King's face; yet the work of His subduing spirit comes on so slowly within me, that I almost doubt it should yet be ready to enjoy the condition of the glorified—

> "I cannot heal, I cannot hide
> My leprosy of sin and pride;
> And were I summoned thus unmeet
> To join the saints on Zion street—
> Now, would my envy knit her frown
> At one who wore a brighter crown;
> And now, my sullen discontent
> Would mar the work o'er which I bent.

> For earthly joys my soul would long,
> Soon weary of the heavenly song—
> The sweet unrest, the holy care,
> The yoke of love, the raiment fair." *

Heaven must be in me, before I can be heaven, and I need the power of the new life to master the sickness of sin. My heart would lift its gates daily that the King of Glory may come in. I want Him "to lodge in the castle, with His mighty captains and men of war, to the joy of the town of Mansoul."† Therefore, on my own account, my prayer shall be daily this, "Thy kingdom come."

2. Let all join in prayer, that the kingdom may *come in the world*. The absolute certainty of the event does not render prayer for its accomplishment the less imperative. The promises were given, not to supersede, but to encourage prayer, and when we turn the promises into prayers, we do but conform to the order between cause and effect, and the end is not more certainly a matter of decree than are the various means to its attainment. When Jehovah promised to "restore the waste places of Judah, and to plant that which was desolate," He subjoined the order, "I will yet for this be inquired of by the house of Israel, to do

---

* G. S. Outram.
Bunyan's "Holy War," chapter ix.

it for them." Just as when He promises bread, it is through the implied use of our hands; when He promises knowledge, it is through the implied use of lessons; when He promises grace, it is through the implied use of the "means of grace;" when He has, in manifold language, assured us that His reign in this world will come, it is implied that it will come through the working of the law of prayer.

The sight of the world's sin in its inveteracy and universality, sometimes makes the lips whiten, and the heart fail. "In the multitude of thoughts" that hold parliament within us, one sceptic thought will sometimes rise to say of the Almighty, "What profit should we have, if we pray to Him?"* Though we go on praying for the kingdom, our spirit is cast down. "How long it is in coming!" we say. A poet sings of God, "His purposes will ripen fast, unfolding every hour." Will they? It seems that, as a matter of fact, they do not. It is now 1883 years ago since Christ was born, yet look at the world! "We see not yet, all things put under Him." We must have patience. "He inhabiteth eternity;" we inhabit only a few years of time. The soul flutters amongst those buds of beautiful purpose, said to "ripen fast," and we think of a butterfly hovering about the buds in a spring garden. Does it

* Job xxi. 15.

fancy that the hard, green sheaths will never burst into flower? Before they do, perhaps the frail little hoverer will shrivel and drop, but for all that, the roses will come out one by one at the right season; so let our impatient spirits be assured, it will be with the promises of the kingdom. Oh, it is coming! although at times the world may be at moments as little like heaven as when it crucified Christ, the reign of the Father is sure in due season to show itself, for no power can ever frustrate His purpose, or falsify His word.

Prayer speaks different languages, takes different forms. Sometimes it takes the form of words, sometimes of gifts, sometimes of actions, sometimes of strenuous fight; and, perhaps, at the moment when in this world the fight has reached its most exciting crisis, and the soldiers of the Cross have done and suffered to their utmost extremity, there may be witnessed one grand and final illustration of the proverb, "Man's extremity, God's opportunity." I look for Christ to come somewhat as His coming is described by the seer of the "Holy War"—in the thick of the battle between Captains Credence and Diabolus. The brave men of Mansoul had fought hard all day outside their walls, to beat back the Powers of Darkness. The battle seemed to waver in the balance. At one time victory seemed to be on the side of Faith, at another on the side of Faith's terrible foe, when, just as the sun was setting, and when the armies were in deadly wrestle, "Captain Credence lifted up his eyes and saw, and behold, Emmanuel came, with colours flying, trumpets sounding, and the feet of his men scarce touching the ground."* "Then the lords of the pit made their escape," and forsook their soldiers, leaving them to fall before the Prince. Over the dead doubters rode the royal army, and the victorious church saluted its victorious Lord. So, let us believe, will Christ come, and thus shall be brought to pass the saying that is written, "The kingdoms of this world are become the kingdoms of our Lord and of His Christ, and He shall reign for ever and ever."

Let us, while striving to learn in the stillness of secret meditation, how to offer aright this prayer when we come into the praying company, think and pray our way from passage to passage deliberately, and with great searching of heart. Before we go on to the next petition, let us pause at this—give time for it to sink into our souls, strike with its own power, and do its own work there. Let us take home the words of John Bradford, the martyr, "When a man shall say, 'Thy kingdom come,' and then shall be thinking with himself, 'Oh, but if it

* "Holy War," chapter xvii.

should now come, what a case I am in!' then, let him not in the midst of these thoughts say, 'Thy will be done on earth as it is in heaven' —so letting the tongue go on with something else before his heart has done with this; but let there be deliberate attendance and careful dwelling on one particular before the next be presented." *

* Quoted from memory.

VI.

THE THIRD PETITION.

"Thy will be done in earth; as it is in heaven."—MATT. vi. 10. "Thy will be done, as in heaven, so on earth."—LUKE xi. 2. *Authorized Version.*

"Thy will be done, as in heaven, so on earth."—MATT. vi. 10. Omitted from the Gospel by Luke. *Revised Version.*

ACCORDING to the revisers, this sentence is given only in St Matthew. His report of the wonderful prayer appears to be the standard; the report in St Luke to be, in some respects, an abridgement; the design of our Lord in this renewed utterance, not being to tell it over again word for word, but to recall the attention of His disciples to it, as to something which they had not properly kept in mind. The second form refers back to the first. Both breathe the spirit of this petition, but the first expresses the spirit in the letter. All who are saying, or trying hard to say, "Thy will be done," may well be thankful still to know that these very words are in the original and complete prayer.

I. What do we mean by this petition?

1. In presenting it, we pray that the will of God may be done by *the will of man*.* Without this as a primary meaning, the prayer is needless, for what would be the use of saying to the omnipotent Sovereign of the universe, "Thy will be done"? As far as He is concerned, it is done already, and ever must be, whether we pray for it or not. "Who hath resisted His will?" "He doeth according to His will in the army of heaven, and among the inhabitants of earth, and none can stay His hand, or say unto Him, What doest thou?"† "I will take the city, whether Zeus wills it or not!" cried the furious Kapaneus, as he rushed up the scaling ladder at the siege of ancient Thebes, but a thunderbolt struck him dead. "I will take Moscow," was the resolve of Napoleon, and when the old saying was cited, "Man proposes, but God disposes," he declared that he intended both to propose and dispose. "Words are but air, and tongues but clay" —we know that, after all, he was defeated, and that the retreat from Moscow was almost a miracle of disaster. While men in the intoxication of absolute power, and in the worship of

---

* Non ut Deus faciat quod vult, sed ut nos facere possimus quod Deus vult."—Cyprian, "De Oratione Dominica."

† Daniel iv. 35.

their own wills, forget their human limitations, and refuse to own a superior, the King of kings is all the while using them as blind instruments, is bending with infinite ease the mightiest and most refractory elements into the service of His own determinations, and is shewing that whether it is man's will or not, His will *must* be done.

Then, is war His will? is ignorance His will? is injustice His will? is misery His will? Is it His will that life should dwindle and pine through filth, neglect, or overcrowding in great cities? Is it His will that infants should die through quieting mixtures and ardent spirits? Is sin His will? Had His will been done when He said to the favoured nation of old, "O that thou hadst hearkened to My commandments! then had thy peace been as a river, and thy righteousness as the waves of the sea"?* "O Jerusalem, Jerusalem, thou that killest the prophets, and stonest them that are sent unto thee, how often would I have gathered thy children together, even as a hen gathereth her chickens under her wings, and ye would not! Behold, your house is left unto you desolate!" †

We have to distinguish between His will of command and His will of control. Included in the fact that on this earth His reign has not yet come, things exist here that are not in

* Is. xlviii. 17.   † Matt xxiii. 37, 38.

accordance with His will of command, and these things, therefore, are simply under His will of control. Failing to see this distinction—holding the hazy creed that somehow, whatever thing happens, it is His will—regarding things as His will which are in reality only obstructions to the free workings of His will—some persons have glided into the habit of mistaking quiescence in evil, for the trance of Christian resignation.

We do the will of God in the sense intended by our Teacher, when, His spirit in our hearts, and His book in our hands, we pay Him our obedience—active obedience to His will as recorded in the words of revelation, passive obedience—that is, the obedience of lowly and patient submission to His will as expressed in the direction or discipline of events. From the nature of this, it must be done willingly. It is by the exercise of God's own will that the material creation obeys Him. He himself sways to unsinning obedience the tides in their beat and the stars in their courses. It is by Himself that His will is done in the happy things of the earth, and air, and water. What child of God cannot enter into the words of one who, years ago, wrote in a time of distress—"The sight of innocent birds in the branches and sheep in the pastures, who act according to the will of their Creator, hath at times tended to mitigate my troubles."* His will is done in the birds, insects, and flowers; but we, who are beings with wills of our own, "are required to do willingly, what the flowers do unconsciously." We, by our own choice, are to spread ourselves out to His light, drink it in, and pour it out again in the beauty and fragrance of holiness. We would not obey His will against our own will, as slaves do, but would be as happy children delighting in the "dear God who loveth us."

"Thy kingdom come; Thy will be done." At first these two petitions seem to be but two forms of one and the same. The second has been called an "amplifying and explicative sentence," repeating the spirit of the first. As we look again, we see a difference. When we say, "Thy kingdom come," the turn of thought is chiefly towards the Father, when we go on to say, "Thy will be done," we are thinking more especially of ourselves, the children. In the one case we pray that He may *rule;* in the other, that we may *bow* to His rule. In the one, we say, "be Thou our gracious king;" in the other, "make us Thy willing people." *In* us, *through* us, *for* us, *over* us,—"Our Father," "Thy will be done." This is our will.

2. This is the prayer of *a renovated* will.

We pray with our *will* that the will of God

* John Woolman.

may be done. Some Christians dimly think that a Christian is to have no will at all, and that the consummation prayed for here, is that our own wills may die, and that the *only* will left living, should be God's. This practically is the doctrine of the monastery, which we may be allowed to illustrate by an oft-told tale from the life of St Francis. The grand rule of his order is the implicit submission of each monk's will to the will of his superior. "One day, a monk proved refractory; his will had to be conquered. 'Dig a grave,' said Francis to the brothers. They dug a grave deep enough to hold a man standing upright. 'Put him into it.' They put him down into it. 'Shovel in the earth.' They did so, while he stood by stern as death. When the mould had reached the victim's knees, the superior bent down, fixed his eyes upon him, and said, 'Are you dead yet?' No answer. Down in that grave stood a man whose will was iron as his own. The signal was given, and the burial went on. Up to the knees, up to the neck, up to the lips the mould was shovelled in. Then Francis bent once more, and said, Are you dead now?' The man in the grave looked up, and saw, in the cold, grey eyes that were fixed upon him, no spark of human feeling. Dead to pity, dead to nature, St Francis stood ready in another moment to give the signal for the complete entombment. Just in time, the iron broke, the will died, the funeral stopped, for the crushed man—a man no longer, because he now had no will, said, 'I am dead,' and was lifted out to join the dead men called monks of the order of St Francis."

That kind of death is not the death gloried in by him who said, "I am crucified with Christ." Man would cease to be man if he ceased to have a will, and God could not be our God if we are dead; for "God is not the God of the dead, but of the living." The death we wish for, is the death not of the will, but of self as its master, through the new and enthroned life of Christ. God's will is that our will should by renovation be more energetically alive than ever, working in harmony with His own. This is what we pray for here. We pray that our own lives and all related lives may be brought into such entire unanimity with God, that what He wills, we may, and that so His will may be done. The great Augustine, speaking of this prayer, tells us that it is another way of saying, "Grant that we may never seek to bend the straight to the crooked, that is, Thy will to ours, but that we, and all doers, may bend the crooked to the straight," our will to Thine, "that Thy will may be done." We do not thus pray naturally. Naturally, we put self, not God in the first place. It is therefore proof of renovation, it is the prayer of children who have been born again, it is the *will* that speaks, and the will all alive with "the power of an endless life."

3. In this prayer to our Father, we say with emphasis, *Thy* will be done.

Here, therefore, in the form of prayer given to us by Jesus Christ, not only for its own literal use, but for use as a directory to prescribe and govern the method and spirit of all prayer and supplication, we are taught to ask for nothing but with the distinct proviso that it accords with the will of God. Before we ask for a single thing on our own account, we lay this foundation stone to build it on, "Thy will be done," and we deliberately pray that our other prayers may be refused if they clash with this. Our real prayer, our ruling prayer, the threefold prayer, out of which as out of a root, all the following prayers are to spring, is, "Hallowed be Thy name, Thy kingdom come, Thy will be done."

This principle has not always received its due prominence. In many minds there is the impression, if not the distinct belief that prayer is simply the request that *our* wills may be done—done in this or that specified particular. The notion often is, that if we do but set our hearts on certain things and offer prayers for them—prayers that are long enough or strong enough—pleading the merits of Christ, "asking in faith, nothing doubting," what we ask for we shall certainly have. The thoughts of some good people are in a tangle about this, and no great injustice is done to their views by the definition thus put by a certain secularist,—" Prayer is a machine, warranted by theologians to make God do what His clients want." After what Christians have sometimes said, we are hardly surprised that in some instances the Christian doctrine has been understood to be that prayer is one of the laws of nature, so that if used by one who understood it, the prayer-power, like any other natural power, must work out certain known and invariable results according to the will of the operator, that will giving sole direction. This led to the well-known challenge made a few years ago by a scientific enquirer: "I ask that one single ward or hospital, under the care of first-rate physicians and surgeons, containing certain numbers of patients afflicted with those diseases which have been best studied, and of which the mortality rates are best known, &c., should be, during a period of not less, say, than three or five years, made the object of special prayer by the whole body of the faithful, and that, at the end of that time, the mortality rates should be compared with the past rates, and also with those of other leading hospitals, similarly well managed during the same space of time."

No test could have been more fair and rational

than this, if we had to regard the question about prayer simply as a disputed principle in natural science. In that case, as after a certain use of the galvanic battery, a shock will follow, so, after certain prayers, we should expect certain answers in the natural order of cause and effect, and we might fairly try prayer in the wards of an infirmary, just as we try quinine, or bark, or any other natural means for making a sick man well.

But prayer is not one of the powers of nature; it is one of the means of grace. It is not like a medical prescription, the efficacy of which is quite irrespective of a right moral spirit of the person who tries it. It is not a mere application to God in language, with whatever confidence in our success. Its power altogether depends on its spirit. While it is an instrument by which God gives good things to His children, it is a process by which He educates them; for thus their souls are brought into sympathy with Himself. We are to ask for nothing but with the understanding that in our receiving it, His will may be done. His will includes obedience, purity, love, and all Christian grace. We are to have the things we pray for, if they are, and if we are in harmony with this. We are in this way fitted to receive the gifts God is waiting to grant, and if not spiritually fitted to receive them, common sense tells us we are better without them.

We disclaim every form and degree of the doctrine that prayer is simply an expedient for getting our own way. Such a theory creates infidels, and its acceptance as true would make prayer itself the ruin of us. It would be fatal to faith in the power of prayer, or in the good of it. Fatal to faith in its power. It is plain that all the prayers prompted simply by the will of man could not be granted. Prayer by some suppliants that certain things may be; by others that they may not be; by some for the success, by others for the defeat of the same cause, could not both be granted at the same time. The prayer of devout Lord Falkland that the king might win, and prayers by the devout Colonel Hutchison that the Parliament might win the same battle, could not have both been granted. Prayers on a sunny day, of certain farmers in a country church that fine weather may last because their hay is down, and prayers of others on the other side of the road that rain may come, because their hay is stocked, and crops of other kinds may be damaged by dry weather, are prayers not likely to be both granted.

But if the unqualified prayers that our own wills may be done, were such that the answer to them would not of necessity imply physical contradictions and impossibilities like these, and if, without reference to the way of the Supreme, you gained by prayer your own way in everything, what would be the effect? What would be the effect on your own child, if you allowed him by prayer to you, to gain his own way in everything? If, while in the nursery, when he cried for a thing, he always had it? If, while still a little one, scarcely able to lisp his wish, he asked for fire, or sharp steel, or explosive chemicals to play with, and had what he asked for? If, when in a fit of industry, he asked leave to weed up all the choice plants in the garden, he had it? If, because his will was against school, he was not sent to school? If, as life went on he could always plead a promise of yours, that he had only to fill up the blank of a cheque according to his own will, and you would always sign it? We need not ask, and indeed such an experiment would be so extreme, that our minds refuse to take in the idea.

Yet you know infinitely less of the great God's thoughts and ways than your nurseling does of yours. For his will to be the rule rather than yours, would be infinitely less disastrous than for your will to be done rather than God's. You will not allow your child to have everything he asks for, simply because it is his will to have it, yet most likely it is the wise law of your house that he should ask you for things he wishes for, when they are beyond the routine of his life, that when he does so, you will if you can, and it is for his good, give him those things; that you will not, as a rule, give them unless he asks, and that you only give them with the understanding that your will is thus done. So the Heavenly Father deals with us. The child asks for what *seems* best. The Father reserves to Himself the right to decide on what *is* best. The child recognizes that right, and says as Jesus did in the garden, "Father, not My will, but Thine be done."

If, indeed, we regarded prayer as "a machine for making God do the will of man," or as a power in nature, like any other such power, sure as law, to take effect according to the will of those who know how to use it; if we sought to change the will of God; if we held the monstrous creed that, by the law of prayer God places his Omnipotence at the disposal of our weakness, so that we could make ourselves or others, rich or poor, well or ill, live or die by our prayers; if we taught that His power could be wielded by man's ignorance, and be subject unconditionally to man's will; if the praying habit which Christ enjoins and Christians practice were such a dangerous instrument, having under the name of a blessing the reality of a curse; we should have no more to say.

As it is, the very act of prayer helps to make our will go along with God's. Each one whose own will has been renovated, is learning to sing—

> "I worship Thee, sweet will of God,
> And all Thy ways adore,
> And every day I live, I long
> To love Thee more and more." *

Some will must be done. Whose? Thy will, our Father! The will of the Best, Wisest, most Holy, most Loving! We adore, we obey, we delight. Ours is not a mere submission to the inevitable, but a choice of the charming, for it is Thy will, the one will that is perfect.

"O Almighty and most merciful God, by Thy bountiful goodness keep us, we beseech Thee, from all things that may hurt us; that we, being ready both in body and in soul, may cheerfully accomplish those things that Thou wouldest have done; through Jesus Christ our Lord. Amen." †

4. We pray that the will of God may be done "on earth as it is in heaven." In the New Version, the substituted phrase, "as in heaven, so on earth," amounts, as far as we can see, to the same thing. Take which rendering you choose, it is not in the nature of an appendix to what has gone before, but is the flower, the very crown and climax, the glory and intensification of the petitions, "Thy will be done." It

* Faber.
† Prayer Book. Collect for the Twentieth Sunday after Trinity.

speaks of the measure and degree in which God's will ought to be done by us—namely, as it is done in heaven. "The measure which Christ lays down for us, is always an infinite measure, and the pattern is always a heavenly pattern." Our heaven is not a mere heaven of the senses. It is the world where God is revealed with most impressive power and most enchanting beauty; and where His will is done —done in creation and in history; done within and without; done in body and in soul, done by all beings, in all ways, to perfection and for ever. The inhabitants of heaven, says Baxter, "obey understandingly, speedily, sincerely, fully, readily, delightedly, unweariedly, and concordantly." "Willingly, speedily, sincerely, fully, and constantly," so responds Archbishop Usher. This is a prayer that the world may be just what it ought to be. It is the very highest ideal of perfection and felicity for the race. Greater thought never dawned on man, grander prayer never rose to God. Only by degrees can we rise to a true conception of its sublimity. It means, let every nation on earth, every province in that nation, every family in that province, every person in that family be saved. Let every house be a temple of God, let every meal be eucharistic, let every man be a priest, and every place be consecrated. Let the Father be revealed through the Son all over the earth,

THE THIRD PETITION.

let every hand bring a tribute; every eye a glance, every voice a song. From every land on which the sunshine strikes, on every shore the ocean laves, let praise softly rise, and sweetly linger.

II. How shall we use this petition? With such applications as the following—

1. Thy will be done *in obedience to orders*. The first meaning is an active one. It speaks of *doing*. Too often this prayer is thought of as a holy sigh; and sounds like a dismal, melting, mournful cadence; an echo to the sobs of Gethsemane; a cry of captives while their harps are hung upon the willows, and tears are mingling with the stream on whose banks they are flung; a plaintive note wafted from some mourner who may hereafter say, "like a crane or a swallow, so did I chatter, I did mourn as a dove;"—a groan from a cowed and exhausted nature; a phrase meaning, "we can do nothing, it is of no use to try, we are very sorry, but,— O God, Thy will be done!"

"Thy will be done." Yes, but the first question is, who should do it? and the answer to this question is, "You." The prayer is not, Thy will be put up with, Thy will be suffered, Thy will be borne as a heavy yoke; but "Thy will be done." It is not, Thy will be thought about, Thy will be cried about, but "Thy will be done." The language is resolute, spirited, full of spring; it has in it the eagerness of the enquiry, "Lord what wilt Thou have me to *do?*" The Lord's life breathed this Lord's prayer. When from the distance of ages He spoke of His advent, He said "I delight to do Thy will O my God;" and "Thy will be done" is the inscription we see displayed over the manger at Bethlehem, over the well of Samaria, and over all the strenuous activities of His obedience no less than over the sorrow in the Garden, and the sacrifice on the Cross.

Let this also be our motto. By making it our prayer we mean that we desire to be "up and doing" in obedience to orders. Our life is all under orders. Because God is our Father to perfection, He is also our King to perfection, and His orders are therefore absolute. Our desire for ourselves is, that we may fall into no mistake about them, that we may clearly know what they are, and then, that we may thoroughly carry them out. We may not always "know the reason why,"—this is not essential; the thing essential to know is, what we have to do, not why we have to do it. The Infinite Reason makes no mistakes, and at every pause of demur, or hint of enquiry, the majestic answer is "what I do, thou knowest not now, but thou shalt know hereafter." Our eyes therefore are on God in Christ, we would wait for a signal from the centre of supreme authority, before we do anything which is not already clear, and we would wait with watchful patience. The son of Antiochus once said, "Father, when will the battle begin?" "Dost thou fear," replied the king, "that thou only in all the army wilt not hear the trumpet?" We are not to act before the commander gives the word, not to delay to act after he has given it, not to be anxious when we have to wait for it. When the time comes for action, the trumpet will give no "uncertain sound;" we shall know what to do,—then, it will be "ours to do or die."

When the steamer *Birkenhead*, with a regiment of soldiers on board, struck upon a rock on the coast of Africa, it was thought from the moment of the first rasp and shock that it could not keep together many minutes, and orders were given to fit the emergency. The roll of the drum called the soldiers to arms on the upper deck. It was promptly obeyed by all, though each one knew that it was his death summons. There they stood, drawn up as in battle-array, looking on while boats were got out, first for the women and children, next for the other passengers—no boats left for them. There they stood firmly and calmly, waiting a watery grave. The ship was every moment going down and down, but there each man stood in his place; the women and children were all got into the boats, and pulled off in safety, but on that solemn deck the soldiers still kept their ranks motionless and silent. Then down went the ship, and down with it went the heroes, shoulder to shoulder, firing a parting volley, and then sinking beneath the remorseless waters; type of spiritual soldiers doing their king's commands, and being "faithful unto death." So may we look to this Book, take our orders from the infinite perfection, and say, living and dying, "Thy will be done!" That it may be so, we would say to the Father what once Augustine did, "Give what thou commandest, and then command what thou wilt."*

2. "Thy will be done" *in submission under trials*. The sorrows that are in the world through sins are used by our Father with sovereign mastery for corrective, or preventive, or educational purposes in his family. Look round in it. There is a father the pride of whose life has been blighted; there is a mother, whose children, for whose life she has offered her own over and over again, are now all buried—buried in the grave, or buried body and soul in business, or buried in the love of some stranger. There is a delicately nurtured being who once lived in a heaven of love and tender praise and beautiful refinement, but who now, in his forlorn old age, had survived all who ever loved him; life has lost its sunny prospects and its cheery stir, and for him in this world there seems to be no future.

* "Da quod jubes, et jube quod vis."

There is another who has been wealthy, but who now, in his decline of strength, has to fight hard for bare bread, or to strain his weary faculties in an attempt to find some way out of a deadlock of difficulties. There is a watcher bending over some dear face with fear, lest in a moment the flame of life should fade, and the white shadow of the grave come over it. There is a thin consumptive coughing his span of life away. It is hard at times for any one of these to say, " Thy will be done ; " hard to say it when the body is a suffering thing, peril to touch, and pain to see ; it is harder still to say it, when the soul itself, still brimful of life, quick as lightning, and impatient of any arrest of its activity in the service of God, is forced to feel that it is the useless and helpless prisoner of the sick body. " His uselessness," as he called it, was the special trial of Archbishop Whately. When, with keen, cool, hard intellect and impetuous energy of will, yet with total exhaustion of body, he lay in his last sickness—" Have you ever preached from the words, ' Thy will be done ? ' said he to his chaplain one day. " How do you explain it ? " When the chaplain replied, " Just so," said he, with choking voice, " but it is hard, very hard, sometimes, to say it ! " Every son of God has his Gethsemane ; his place for the cup of bitterness and the prayer of agony. Although there can be no atoning element in what we go through, and our cross never can be that of sacrifice, we may have a cross in the very prospect of which our soul is "exceeding sorrowful." Then it is right for us to pray as he did, "Father, if it be possible, let this cup pass from me." We may in this case kneel where he knelt, and say what he said, but we may not divide his words; we must add that hard word "*nevertheless*," and say in prospect of the unknown trouble, "Thy will be done." After *that* prayer we are ready for the cross, if one is waiting for us, or able to live through the affliction that may be our cross just now. By the help of the Comforter, the promises that shine out in our sorrows, as stars shine out in the night, encourage us to offer this prayer; we are encouraged to offer it by the memory of what God has done for us. "Do you know *this*, Master Cameron?" said an executioner, startling the old Christian in his cell, and showing something in a basket. It was a fair-haired youthful head, just stricken off. "I know it, I know it. My son's—my own dear son's. It is the Lord; good is the will of the Lord, who cannot wrong me nor mine, but has made goodness and mercy follow us all our days." The same goodness and mercy have followed ours, warranting the same trust in the same blessed will. It is the will of One who cannot wrong us, the will of our "Father in Heaven." "'God is Love,' is the motto on the weather-cock of a country friend. We have seen many curious vanes, but never one that struck our attention so much as this, 'God is Love.' Our friend was asked if he meant to imply that the love of God was as fickle as the wind? 'No,' he answered, 'I mean that which ever way the wind blows, God is Love; if cold from the north, or biting from the east, still God is Love, as much as when the warm south, or genial west wind refreshes our fields and flocks.' Yes, so it is! our God is always Love. We saw our friend the other day, when he had lost his dearly loved wife, but amidst his heartache and crushing loss, he still said, 'My vane teaches me the truth; I put over it in my prosperity when the desire of my eyes was at my side—God is *Love.*'"* Can we not yet trust Him enough to say in our cares and pains, "Thy will be done!"

3. "Thy will be done" by *surrender to Thy guidance.* Those mysterious travellers, our souls, have paths before them of which they know nothing. The map of their future is a secret hid away amidst the glories of God. What we shall want, what and where our dangers will be, how long we shall be on the road, and at what part of it we shall find heaven, no prophet has been commissioned to disclose. We need that the Father's will should

* Rev. C. H. Spurgeon

steer and guide our life, and that for all the future we should trust Him totally; yet sometimes we hardly let ourselves go, or let those dear as ourselves go, out from our seeing or keeping. We try to make out some glimmering outline of things to come; we try to reserve some power of choice as to the course, or as to the stations of our pilgrimage. We are like Joseph, when he took his two children to receive a blessing from his father. "And Joseph took them both, Ephraim in his right hand toward Israel's left hand, and Manasseh in his left hand toward Israel's right hand, and brought them near to him. And Israel stretched out his right hand and laid it on Ephraim's head, who was the younger, and his left hand upon Manasseh's head, guiding his hands wittingly, for Manasseh was the first-born." * God was the arbiter of the hands. His will moved in the movement of the blind old man. It was of no use then, it is of no use now, trying to guide the Guide. Let Him lead; let us follow. We find, for the most part, that when we have been suffered to have our way, rather than His way in scheming for the future, we have worked out some disaster, and that when our burning prayers to be led in some particular direction pointed out by ourselves, have been refused, that refusal has proved itself to be in the long

* Genesis xlviii. 13, 14.

run, an act of wisest mercy calling for loudest praise.

Monica prayed that the Lord would bring her dear son Augustine to the knowledge of himself; she also prayed that He would keep him from voyaging, as he had purposed to do, from Africa to Italy. After all he went to Italy, and the loving suppliant was in trouble because her prayers were not heard. Yet, being at Milan, going to hear Ambrose preach, and thinking only to be charmed by the magic of his eloquence, he found "the pearl of great price," and began his great life of Christian service,—with reference to which fact he has said, "Thou O good God, deep in counsel, and hearing the substance of my mother's desires, didst not regard what she *then* asked, that in me Thou mightest do that which she ever asked." * This clause of the Lord's prayer, as applied to guidance in all our future, amounts to saying, as to time or place, health or sickness, life or death, and all possibilities. "Lord, what Thou wilt, where Thou wilt, when Thou wilt." †

4. "Thy will be done," in *the use of means for thy reign to come.*

Amidst the solemn glories of a famous French Cathedral, stands a statue that represents a man speaking. One hand grasps a crucifix, the

* Confess. Lib. v. 8. † Baxter's last words.

other is lifted as if with the life and sway of passionate oratory; and below his feet, sculptured on the massive pedestal, are the words, "Thy will be done." That stands for Peter the Hermit, the fire of whose appeals kindled the first crusade. "Never, perhaps," says Dean Milman, "did single speech of man work such extraordinary results. He made the people feel that to get the Holy Sepulchre from the Saracens, was the will of God, and before the council closed, the one loud cry from it broke forth, 'it is the will of God, it is the will of God!'" We want the crusader's enthusiasm, without the crusader's mistakes. We want deep conviction alive with Pentecostal flame, when will men rush with equal ardour to fight the true battles of the true cross!

Sometimes it is His will that to help on this cause, you should part with what you would naturally like to keep. Sometimes that your own selves should go into the battlefield of Christian missions, when you would naturally like to stay at home; sometimes that you should part with son or daughter ordained by Him for such high service. Perhaps at this very moment, and in reference to one of these very intimations of the divine will, you are saying, "Thy will be done," but in what sense? Is it true for instance that your child is going, and that you are saying this in the mere spirit of resignation. It should rather be in the spirit of obedience. It should mean on your part, not a suffering, but a doing. The beautiful "living sacrifice," is about to be made ; honestly, heartily, take your part in it. You have held back your consent till now, but now you give up and say, "Thy will be done!" Do it, *do* it, brother, sister, will you not? Do it yourself, not content to have it done for you!

VII.

THE FOURTH PETITION.

"Give us this day our daily bread."—MATT. vi. 11. "Give us day by day our daily bread."—LUKE xi. 3. *Authorised and Revised Versions.*

WHEN our minds are saturated with the spirit of the foregoing words—when our hearts are full of the life that says, "Our Father which art in heaven, Hallowed be Thy name, Thy kingdom come, Thy will be done on earth, as it is in heaven,"—when we have the thorough understanding that our desires are to be fenced within these holy limits,—and that what we ask on our own account is to be ruled by the law of subordination thus declared, then we begin to pray for ourselves, and this is our first petition— "Give us this day our daily bread."

In making out its true meaning, we propose to pause at each leading word or phrase in it, giving emphasis to each, successively.

I. We put emphasis on the phrase "Daily Bread."

"Daily." The original word, it is well-known, is nowhere else found, either in sacred or classical literature. It is conjectured that Matthew and Luke coined it, as a translation of the Aramaic phrase used by our Lord. More than thirty different explanations of it have been suggested, and the revisers make no attempt to settle its derivation or meaning. As, however, grammarians have found much to say for the rendering, "our bread for the coming day," they have, in both evangelists, inserted this in the margin, but have retained in the text, the word "daily,"—the translation to which we have been accustomed. The word in the Greek Testament, whatever may have been its history, appears to be a compound of a noun meaning "substance," with the preposition.* As applied to bread, it seems to mean, that which is proper or sufficient for supporting life by being changed into the *substance* of our bodies. It seems to stand for good and nourishing food. Though it may be impossible to give it a literal translation, our conclusion is, that the general spirit and meaning of the term *daily* bread must be accepted as correct.

"Bread." The word is most simple, yet most comprehensive. It includes, we think, several things. In the statement of its mean-

* According to this, ἐπιούσιον is compounded of ἐπι and ὀυσία, substance, or subsistence. An instance of this word occurs in Luke xv. 12, τὸ επιβάλλον μερος της ὀυσίας. Tholuck has given a long, full and very fair account of the reasons offered for the rendering in the margin and that adopted in our English text, but sums up in favour of the latter.

ing, we must begin at the lowest point, and ascend.

1. "Bread" means that which is needful to support *the life of the body*. This, surely, is not restrictively the food that comes from corn, but the food that our bodies live upon, whatever that may be. The Arab who may live upon dates gathered from the tree; the Indian, who may live upon food got by gun or net, or spear; the man whose food grows in the field; the man who earns it by toiling brain or by skilful fingers—every man, however he gets his living, is invited to offer this prayer, and in praying for "bread" prays for the usual supports of material existence.

Some interpreters understand the petition as having reference only to the bread of the soul. Their theory is, that the wants of the body are beneath the notice of God, and unworthy of a place in the train of supplications taught by Christ. They are afraid or ashamed to "trouble the Master" about such a trifle! The earlier divines generally clung to a spiritual interpretation, and even Luther tells us that this is a request to be fed by the Bread of Heaven. But this cannot be the only idea. We have no proof that the half of man's nature, though it be the lower half, is disowned by Him who made it. It is no "counsel of perfection," whatever ascetics teach, that our souls are to starve or trample out the instincts of our bodies. There was no neglect of the body in Paradise. No such neglect is taught by the theology of Nature or by the standing lessons of "seed time and harvest." He who made the body, will not scorn to feed it. He, who, though Lord of all, stooped under the lowly lintel of this, our "cottage of clay," and dwelt in a body like our own for more than thirty years; He who gave bread to the multitudes by the hand of miracle; He who pronounced a blessing on bread before taking it with His disciples; He who in many ways in His human teachings, sanctified the mystery of food; He who has taught each believer that His body is a temple of the Holy Ghost; He who guards it in the darkling decay of the grave, so that no mystic atom, essential to its continuous identity shall be lost and missing on the resurrection day—stoops to no degradation, and speaks in no way unlike Himself, by teaching us to pray for it, and we, the children of God, feel that any interpretation is quite unnatural as well as unscriptural that would deprive us of the great privilege of casting our bodily wants in this simple prayer, upon our Heavenly Father.

2. The bread we pray for includes that which is needful to support *all our life* in *this world*. This is manifold more than the life of the body. Our life is compound, made of earth and heaven,

dust from the ground, and breath from Deity. It is even more than this, for it must mean the life suitable to the particular station we have to fill. Daily bread in the sense of needful support to the life which fills a large sphere, daily bread for the life on which many other lives depends, daily bread for the life that needs property and social influence to fulfil the functions of its place, is totally different from that which is wanted to feed the life of a mere human unit, just alive. Prince and peasant, parent and child, persons of every estate, with all varieties of claims upon them, little or great, few or many, are all alike to ask the Father in heaven for daily bread, but bread for the Queen does not mean merely a loaf a day. Bread for the poor old mother by the cottage fire does not mean supplies enough to meet the demands of empire. The bread we are to ask for, is support for our differing lives of body, of mind, of work, of trial, of office, of station and responsibility.

3. Prayer for "daily bread" is prayer that we may have *enough*. The word "bread" points to what is simple and moderate. We have no encouragement to say give us this day a banquet. There is nothing to make us think that the means of faring sumptuously every day are to be had for asking. We are only to ask for supplies that shall meet the average, inevitable demands of life and station; the spirit of this is that of Agur's prayer, "feed me with food convenient

for me;" but while the words forbid extravagance they imply a request for sufficiency, and in making them our own we ask for enough to keep life in healthy, happy, growing power.

If we rebel against God's plan of our life; if our hearts clamour for more than enough of life's good things; if we insist on having whatever hits our fancy, feeds our pride or delights our senses, we are on dangerous ground. The sovereign may indeed hear the prayer of discontent, but in that case the answer to a prayer may be but the infliction of a curse. When his typical people were passing through the desert, though he gave them daily bread, they passionately longed for something more. "He had rained down manna upon them to eat, and had given them of the corn of heaven. Man did eat angels' food: he sent them meat to the full."* But they pined for variety; wept, and said, "who shall give us flesh to eat?" Then the Royal message to their leader was—" Say thou unto the people, sanctify yourselves against tomorrow, and ye shall eat flesh: for ye have wept in the ears of the Lord, saying who shall give us flesh to eat? for it was well with us in Egypt: therefore the Lord will give you flesh, and ye shall eat. Ye shall not eat one day, nor two days, nor five days, neither ten days, nor twenty days," but even for a whole month?

* Psalm lxviii. 24, 25.

Our thoughts flash back into that ancient scene, and in a moment, we seem to be living in it. It is a still day in the burning depth of the wilderness; no shadow flits across the glare; no sound, near or far, strikes upon the velvet carpet of the sand. All at once, man after man starts up and listens. A noise like a loud whispering hangs in the air; it comes nearer, like wind in trees, nearer and nearer till it sounds like the roar and hiss of a storm in the sails of a ship at sea. The sunshine changes into sudden darkness; you look up; and see birds, and more birds, gathering overhead, till they are wedged into a black, dense quivering cloud; they drop down on low, weary wing, and fall in stacks all round the camp; the people run in a rage of delight to snatch and rend them; but not being prepared for so sudden a change of regimen, and not being temperate, the new food turns into poison, and they take into the system, not life but death. "So the Lord smote the people with a very great plague, and he called the name of that place the graves of lust, because there they buried the people that lusted."* "Now," says our inspired expositor of this episode, "these things happened unto them by way of example; and they were written for our admonition, upon whom the ends of the ages are come."†

* Numbers xi. 33, 34. † 1 Cor. x. 11.

THE FOURTH PETITION.

II. We would now separate the phrase "Give us," that we may think over its special meaning.

1. This phrase implies *acknowledgment of dependence*. It amounts to this, Father, *give us* our daily bread, or we shall never have it. Our personal and unceasing dependence on Him for the supports of mere existence is a fact that few would formally question, but which, perhaps, few adequately feel. We seem to need the rack of material circumstance to work a present, pending, urgent sense of it. When our lips confess it, sometimes our souls are silent; it is more like a dead word in a book, than a word alive within us. "Give us this day our daily bread," is a prayer we are ready to say, fit for the helpless sufferer who has just broken into his last shilling, but is it natural to the man whose "barns are filled with plenty," to the prosperous merchant who has just contracted to furnish a fleet with stores, or to the lord of large estates? It might have fitted the lips of David in the day when, starving, he asked the priest for a fragment of the shew-bread; but would it have been suitable to Solomon in all his glory? Would it have been the natural language of Job, in the days of health, wealth, and happy family festival? Would it have been proper for Joseph when opening the granaries in which he had stored the produce of seven plenteous years? Yes, verily, for all alike live on gifts,

and in "the fulness of sufficiency" one fire, one blight, one hurricane, one shipwreck, one rash venture, one turn in the tide of affairs, the work of one idiotic head, or of one random hand, may in a week bring the highest to the level of the lowest. In our grand impatience of common places, we are tempted to slight these simple truths, and to forget them because we think they are too obvious to be forgotten. Let us not be too proud to take them in with new and keen realization, remembering not only our equal dependence, but who it is on whom we depend. He who of old sent the manna down: He who sent the ravens with food for Elijah, He who guided the quivering shoal of fishes like living, leaping, lighted gold and silver, straight into Peter's net; is still the sovereign Lord of mine and mountain, of field and forest, of sea and sand. So thought the Puritan Fathers of America, who while eking out their scanty supplies of food in their first years with the shell-fish of the shore, thanked the Lord, with beautiful reverence, for showing them "the treasures hid in the sand." So think we, while we offer this prayer in spirit and truth.

2. We say to our Father, "give us" this blessing, because we know that it is His nature to give, and that *giving is His delight*. If we think of Him as of one who gives, but who would rather not give; who gives with grudging, and

who counts out with cold, slow, reluctant fingers what he gives; who gives only when we passionately beg and pray, and who likes to say No to us,—no words can measure the wrong we do to Him or to ourselves. The joy of possessing is in the power of giving, and this is the joy of the Lord. Unless in some work of judgment —"His strange work," we never see God, but as we see Him giving. For ever working to propel the sleepless forces that beat and throb through nature—the soft drops, the quickening airs, the searching rays, that make the swelling leaf, the filling ear, the reddening fruit, we see Him for ever giving exquisitely, variously and with magnificent munificence, "seed to the sower and bread to the eater."

In connection with gifts for the support of existence, think of His gifts for its enjoyment. James Hamilton said, if this world had been meant as a place for the bare physical life of man during his allotted time, "a world less beautiful would have served the purpose.... A big, round island, half of it arable, and half of it pasture, with a clump of trees in one corner, and a magazine of fuel in another, might have held and fed ten millions of people; and a hundred islands, all made on the same pattern, big and round, might have held and fed all the populations of the globe. There was no need for the carpet of verdure or the ceiling of blue; no need for the mountains, and cataracts and forests; no need for the rainbow, no need for the flower."

Look at the gift of flowers only. There are in this world, wildernesses of beauty, where you see rich mists of flowers, vast sweeps and stretches of flowers, flowers billowing round the tree stems, rippling rivers of flowers, tossing cataracts of flowers, prairies, where you may travel to-day, to-morrow and the day after, still through nothing but flowers. Wherever nature can get air and space enough, even in our duller landscapes, we may see something like it. Graces of shape and glorious fires of colour are wherever they can be, and even a wreath of snow is a bank of flowers, with tiny stars of loveliness full of wonders. What a noble, generous, resplendent King our Father is! Everywhere, in illuminated letters, we read the motto of His house, "Enough and to spare." Never let us make our requests to Him, as if taking a liberty or expecting a denial, for He delights to give.

3. We mean give us this *for Thou art our Father*. We see Him delighting to give to countless creatures that have not His Spirit in them, and of whom He is not Father. Give *us* our bread. Why, He gives the birds *theirs!* He puts His living law and His subtle skill within them; He infuses into them the life that, while

in happy movement, singing happy songs, is in perpetual happy quest for the food which He gives them through stream and tree and air, and what He gives, they gather. It seems that sparrows, above all the other birds, are the selected types to teach lessons of His providence —the little, saucy, dingy London sparrows, chirping close about us, not scared by our stirs nor stifled by our smoke, are our Saviour's messengers reminding us of His words, that not even one of them is forgotten before God, and that we "are of more value than many sparrows." Shall He clothe His lilies and forget His saints, feed His sparrows and starve His children? You know a father's feelings. Even you "who are evil" do not think that what is needful for the earthly life of your child is too small a thing for you to care about, and can you dream that God in heaven does not care if His children are cold and hungry? Doubt of that, is doubt that He is your Father.

4. We mean "Give us" our daily bread through a blessing on our own use of *right* means. One evening, we are told, Mahomet was conversing with his followers, and overheard one of them say, "I will *loose* my camel, and trust;" on which he said, "Friend, *tie* thy camel, and trust." Do whatever is yours to do, then trust. Work and trust, watch and pray. "If a man will not work, neither shall he eat," is a law of the kingdom. Work done, all is done that man need

care about, God will care for the rest. In reference to daily bread, the faith that is without care is expressed in unwearied activity, as a dutiful fulfilment of the little as well as the great obligations of life and time. "The man who thinks Providence exists simply to make up his lack of service, despises Providence."* In ordinary circumstances, God gives in ordinary ways, and this prayer, translated into the language of practical life, mainly means—"Father, give us work to do, and strength to do it." The *work* must be His gift, as well as the bread which it brings. That work which God does not give, and which is therefore without the sanction of His holiness or the blessing of His love; work not in harmony with the three first petitions of this model, work done in the spirit of the gambler, work that implies any form of social injustice, work of those who "make haste to be rich;" work that makes capital out of social sin of others, or that panders to destructive passions— for instance, the opium traffic and the like— work of men who "fish foul bread out of the standing pools and the slimiest ooze of human depravity," who dip their daily morsel in that which is the poison of human hearts, who make a profit out of lost souls, and who bequeath to their children the gains of unrighteousness,— work of that kind, whatever its connection and

* Fairbairn

whatever its degree, has no prosperity from heaven, and the bread that comes of it is not God's gift. In the spirit of this prayer we ask Him to give us the means of supporting life lawfully and honourably, and to give us working faculties. If we live by the skill of our fingers, we ask Him to give us this skill; if by the sight of our eyes, to let no curtain of darkness fall over them; if by strength of limbs, to let no evil strike that strength; if our minds have to work, that our minds may be kept from weakness or eclipse, that so, giving us these, He may give us our daily bread.

5. Another thought under this language is, "Our Father, when common means are not within our power. 'Give us' our daily bread, *by means of thine own.*" When every door is shut, every road blocked up, and we are at a loss, come to our help by the ordinations of thy mysterious providence. We see with God, no waste of power, no needless profusion of contrivance; miracles are not sights for every day, but when all the dutiful and necessary things that we know of have been done on our own part, we may say, "it is time for thee, O Lord, to work." Powerless to stir another step, although in the way of his appointment, a Voice will say "stand still, and see the Salvation of the Lord." "He reserves His hand," says a Puritan sage, "for a dead-lift" The stories of our fathers' lives are

rich with proofs of this. Nathaniel Lawrence, ejected from the living of Baschurch in 1662, sat one day under a hedgerow, thinking of his hungry family. What suddenly made his eye flash and his foot spring? The sight of a shilling in the ditch, seeming to him, so he said, to have dropped straight out of heaven.

Oliver Heywood, ejected from Coley Vicarage by the act of uniformity, lived on a little stock of savings, until one day, he and his children were at starvation point, and with no earthly prospect of another meal. They sang at family prayer—

> "When cruse and barrel both are dry
> We still will trust the Lord most High."

With empty purse and empty basket, their faithful old servant then set out from the house, and wandered through the streets of Halifax, thinking of the famishing children whom she loved like her own life, and wondering how God would give them this day their daily bread. Returning home, one of the tradespeople of the place, standing at his door, knew her, called her in, and told her that he was just casting about for a messenger to take a remittance of five guineas just sent him from Manchester from the master. On her arrival home with money and food, it looked like a miracle, and the father said, when they met at evening prayer—"The Lord hath not forgotten to be gracious. His word is true from the beginning. "The young lion *may* lack and suffer hunger, but they that trust the Lord shall not lack any good thing."*

III. We would next place emphasis on the word "Our," in this connection. We only ask for *our* bread, not for the bread belonging to others. One man is not to have more than his share, or to live on that which ought to support another man's life. A workman, high or low, lives on bread not his own, when he takes a fair day's wages without a fair day's work. A master takes bread not his own, when he takes a fair day's work without a fair day's wages. It is, then, sin of any man who, while below the horizon of solvency, carries on trade by false shows and fictitious values; who wears another man's coat, drives another man's carriage, lives in another man's house, calling what he thus appropriates his own. "We are to ask for our *own* bread, and we are not allowed to ask the bread of others—we must not covet our neighbour's goods, but must be content with what God gives us in the way of honest industry, or by the kindness of our friends." †

IV. We would next dwell on the power of the phrase "This day."

---

* Dr Fawcett's "Life of Heywood."

† Dr John Brown's "Discourses and Sayings of our Lord," Vol. I., p. 246.

Matthew Henry, talking in his own quaint, racy, simple style, like an old father to the children round his chair, says, "The Lord's prayer is a letter sent from earth to heaven. Here, in the inscription of the letter, is the name of the Person to whom it is directed, 'Our Father;' the place *where*, "which art in heaven." The *contents* of it in several *errands of request*. The *seal* 'Amen,' and if you will, the *date*, 'this day.'"

The distinct instruction of our Lord in the first announcement of this prayer, that we are to use the words "this day," goes far to prove that the marginal rendering of another term in the same verse, is wrong.* The original word in question, and which is represented in our English New Testament by the word "daily," may, indeed, be possibly traced to a root which would admit of being represented under the phrase "bread of to-morrow," as in the margin. This is uncertain, for critics are divided in opinion. The rule in the words "this day" is a *certainty*, and we never allow a certainty to be ruled by an *un*certainty. The request, "Give us this day the bread of to-morrow," would be scarcely intelligible, and to adopt it without necessity, would be, without necessity to turn a plain thing into a puzzle. We cannot admit a rendering that would contradict or

" Our bread for the coming day."

nullify the power of the phrase "this day," as reported by Matthew, or the extension of the same petition in the report by Luke, in which we are taught to ask for supplies one day at a time—that is, "day by day."

The Lord of Life would not indeed have us live only in the present, and have no readiness for the future. The whole tendency of His grace is to secure that readiness. But while under the law of the prayer, "thy will be done," we lay our plans for to-morrow, we are not to be distracted by the fear of to-morrow. This is the dread spectre which the Master's language is to lay, the wearing care which He seeks to tranquillize. In the discourse following the first publication of the sacred prayer, He says, "Take no thought for your life, what ye shall eat, neither for your body, what ye shall put on, is not the life more than meat, and the body than raiment?" In this tender strain He goes on to the close, when He says, "Take therefore no thought for the morrow; for the morrow shall take thought for the things of itself. Sufficient unto the day is the evil thereof."*

---

* Matthew vi. 26, *ad finem*. In Luke's report of a similar discourse of our Lord (Luke xii. 29), we find after the charge "Seek not ye what ye shall eat or what ye shall drink," the words "neither be ye of doubtful mind. μὴ μετεωρίζεσθε. "Be not poised in suspense, unable to settle to anything."

All this chapter on Providence is in the spirit of the words "give us this day our daily bread." This day, Christians, is the only day you are living in. Perhaps it requires all the faith you can exercise, and all the strength you can strain, to live it well. You have no overplus of ability. If you bring into this day, the care that belongs to to-morrow; if you try to look to-day at the scenery of to-morrow; if you try this day to cross the bridge of to-morrow; if, this day, being at the foot of the hill, you try to see over the crest of it, which you propose to reach to-morrow; if you try to load to-day with the pack of to-morrow, you weaken to-day. You not only attempt an impossibility, but you live over your troubles twice, before they come, and when they come. Even the Arabs rebuke you by their proverb, "The bread of to-morrow, to-morrow." Your days are already provided for; each day, as each day comes. The standing promise, "as thy days, so thy strength shall be," gives perpetual inspiration to the prayer that we may have *this* day what the day's necessities require. *This* day, whatever the day may be; *this* day, whether day of peace or day of storm, *this* day, living day, or dying day, for we depend on Him one day as much as on another.

From the nature of this prayer, the date must be "this day." "Prayer is the Christian's vital breath." We do not live to-day by virtue of

THE FOURTH PETITION.

our breathing *yesterday;* we must not put off our breathing until *to-morrow.* We must breathe to-day or die. As bread is the support of life, we want bread to-day that we may live to-day.*

V. This petition *suggests a higher petition.*

The grace of Christ is, in the symbolical language of Scripture, so frequently compared by food, that we are not surprised to find nearly all the primitive expositors adopting some modification or other of the view that it involves a prayer for the nourishment of the higher life of the spirit, over and above the material substance.† This is not our view; but while we regard it as a petition only for the supplies needful for our life in this world, and while we are comforted by the thought that our Heavenly Father cares for our bodies as well as our souls, the cry to Him for those earthly supports which we sum up under the term "bread," irresistibly *suggests* a prayer for heavenly bread. It is one thing to say it prescribes, another that it suggests this. The

---

* "Our bread, though in itself stale and mouldy as that of the Gibeonites, is every day new, because a new and hot blessing, as I may say, is daily begged and bestowed of God upon it." Thomas Fuller, "Meditations on all kinds of prayer." —Sect. xv. "He who has what he needs for to-day, and says what shall I eat to-morrow? has not faith. He who creates the day, creates the food for it."—Talmud, quoted by Dr Gill

† "Panis superstantialis."

spiritual mind will from "the meat that perisheth," naturally rise in thought to "the meat that endureth to everlasting life.*

We say with Sir Matthew Hale, "O Lord Thou didst at first freely give me my being. I could not deserve it when I was not; the same title that I have to my being I have to my preservation and support of my being; it is still free gift, and therefore I come to Thee for my bread upon no other terms than as a poor beggar to a bountiful Lord. . . . Give me, I pray, bread for this day, and when to-morrow comes, I will beg bread of Thee for to-morrow. . . . But above all, ever give me the Bread of Life, that whilst my body is fed, my soul may not be starved, either for the want of that everlasting Bread, or for want of an appetite for it."

This Bread can only be ours as a gift. Our life must be one perpetual prayer for it. God is always giving, we are always receiving, so both the gift and the life supported by it, we have "renewed day by day." The clause of the Lord's Prayer which we are now upon, was read by the Anglo Saxons, thus—"Our daily loaf sell us to day." † The word *sell* has, in the course of its history passed through a change of meaning, but not a few are ready to take the

---

* " He who uses this petition would do well to keep both in view."—Adam Clarke.

† " Urne dægwamtican hlāf syle us to-dæg "

old word in its modern meaning, and so to use it when they ask God for earthly or heavenly bread.

One sharp winter day, so runs a nursery tale, a poor woman stood at the window of a king's conservatory, looking at a cluster of grapes, which she longed to have for her sick child. She went home to her spinning wheel, earned half-a-crown, and offered it to the gardener for the grapes. He waved his hand, and ordered her away. She returned to her cottage, snatched the blanket from her bed, pawned it, and once more asked the gardener to sell her the grapes, offering him five shillings. He spoke furiously to her and was turning her out, when the princess came in, heard the man's passion, saw the woman's tears, and asked what was wrong. When the story was told she said "my dear woman, you have made a mistake. My father is not a merchant, but a king; his business is not to sell but to give;" so saying, she plucked the cluster from the vine and dropped it into the woman's apron.

All good things from God are gifts. "Gratis" is written on every one, but most vividly of all on this. Do you ask "how much?" Do you dream that salvation is for sale? Can God sell pardon? sell a new heart? sell love? sell righteousness? sell strength? sell any or all of the things included in what we call grace? It is a gift, and you can give nothing for a gift. You may, however, ask for it, indeed you must. To say "you have the promise, but you must pray for its fulfilment," is only as if a man should say to a man, "you shall have the cheque cashed, but you must first present it." Every day offer with this application, the petition, " Give us this day our daily bread," then every day you will have it, and have it in sufficiency. God in Christ is saying to each suppliant, "My grace is sufficient," that is, enough "for thee," and each suppliant may have in his heart the spirit of the answering words—

> "Thou art enough, O Lord, for all my sin,
> Enough to cleanse me and to keep me clean;
> All down life's pathway, lone, or dark, or rough,
> Thou art enough, O Lord, Thou art enough.
>
> Thou art enough in days of light and gladness,
> Enough in days of sickness and of sadness;
> Enough, when standing on death's solemn shore,
> Always enough—enough for ever more"

VIII.

THE FIFTH PETITION.

"And forgive us our debts, as we also forgive our debtors."
—MATT. vi. 12. *Authorized Version.*

"And forgive us our sins; for we also forgive every one that is indebted to us."—LUKE xi. 4. *Authorized Version.*

"And forgive us our debts as we also have forgiven our debtors."—MATT. vi. 12. *Revised Version.*

"And forgive us our sins, for we ourselves also forgive every one that is indebted to us."—LUKE xi. 4. *Revised Version.*

I. OBSERVE how this petition *begins*. "*And* forgive us our debts." This is not the only instance in the Record of an important passage which has "and" for the significant opening word. The ninth chapter of Matthew's gospel begins in the middle of a sentence. The first word in it is "and." Like a coupling chain that links together two carriages, it links the two chapters together into one consecutive train of history. The last verse of one chapter is—"The whole city came out to meet Jesus; and when they saw Him, they besought Him that He would depart out of their coasts." The first verse of the next, is, "*And* He entered into a ship, and passed over, and came into His own city." The word "and" is the sign of connection between the two statements. The people wished Christ to go away, "and" He went away. We might name other instances from the same "Book of the Lord" in which the word "and" is introductory, in which also, though scarcely a word at all, it is used to carry a momentous meaning.

This clause of the divinely given prayer begins with the same conjunction. Christ uses no waste words, and be sure this is not one. It marks the connection and fixes the order between this and the preceding request. "Forgive us our sins," fitly follows, "give us this day our daily bread." Even life would not be a boon if not connected with pardon. When the great Inspirer gives continuous life through the continuous gift of that which feeds it, we find to our sorrow, that in this world, the life thus given goes wrong—it is always sinning, and therefore, always needing forgiveness.

II. A second peculiarity of this prayer is, that it is a prayer for the forgiving of our sins *as the children of God*. Not as outcasts, not as prisoners of war, not as lost sinners, or as sentenced convicts, but as *Christians* do we thus pray. It is in fact a prayer for the forgiveness of those who have *already been forgiven*. The statement may

THE FIFTH PETITION. 181

seem to involve a contradiction. How shall we declare this parable?

Our sins as rebels have already been forgiven. From the happy moment when we became "the children of God by faith in Jesus Christ," we were forgiven the sins committed through all the days of our unregeneracy, and on account of which we had been condemned to die. Of this forgiveness the Spirit of the Most High speaks to us in metaphors intended to suggest a greatness that is beyond mortal comprehension. "As far as the east is from the west, so far hath He removed our transgressions from us."* What calculus can help us to find out how far that is? "Thou hast cast all my sins behind Thy back."† Though this was said in the rapture of poetry, the poetry of Scripture can only speak the soul of truth, and how far out of sight is that which is behind the Infinite? "Thou wilt cast all their sins into the depths of the sea."‡ How far down are the depths of that mystic sea? All these are terms of infinity, and created faculties will never grasp the greatness of the reality they indicate. In the day of our surrender, our sins as rebels, were forgiven with such total and absolute completeness, that all the forgiving power of infinite love could not make them more forgiven than they are. The fact stuns us with its wonderfulness, it seems too glorious

* Psalm ciii. 12.   † Isaiah xxxviii. 17.
‡ Micah v. 19.

to be true; long after our Father has clasped us to His heart, and welcomed us to His home, there are times when, as if He had not spoken one word of hope, we find ourselves still asking Him to forgive us the sins of the life we wasted in "the far country," as well as the sins committed since our welcome home, when it was said over each of us, "this my son was dead and is alive again, was lost and is found!" For years after Dr Donne had been "accepted in the Beloved," he implored pardon for his old sins of rebellion, pouring out his anguish in this piteous cry :—

"Wilt Thou forgive that sin where I begun,
   Which was my sin, though it were done before?
Wilt Thou forgive that sin through which I run
   And do run still, though still I do deplore?
When Thou hast done, Thou hast not done,
      For I have more.

"Wilt Thou forgive that sin which I have wonne
   Others to sin, and made my sins their own,
Wilt Thou forgive that sin which I did shun
   A year or two, but wallowed in a score?
When Thou hast done, Thou hast not done,
      For I have more.

'I have a sinne of fear, that when I've spun
   My last thread, I shall perish on the shore;
But swear by Thyself, that at my death Thy Son
   Shall shine as he shines now, and heretofore?
And having done that, Thou hast done;
      I fear no more."*

  * Dr. John Donne, 1635. Donne's Poems, vol. ii. p. 341. Grosart's Fuller Worthies.

Like this old poet, many Christians are still asking the forgiveness of sins from the charge of which they were cleared for ever, when, being justified by faith, they crossed the line from the lost to the saved state, they use up in needless lamentations the life that is wanted for urgent service, and their hearts melt with the misery of doubt while they have a right to all the joy that rings in our triumphant challenge. It is God that justifieth; who is he that condemneth?"

In full gladness of assent to this, and as we think, in perfect consistency with it, our creed is, that even *after* the grand, initial forgiveness which is included in our "justification," and which is coincident with the birth within us of everlasting life—that is, even after we have been "born again," although we are children of God, we are for the present, sinful children. "There is not a just man upon earth, that doeth good and sinneth not." "It is a shame that it should be so," remarks Andrew Fuller, "but so it is. To disown it, makes the matter, not better, but worse. This direction of Christ contains an insuperable objection to the notion of those deluded people who imagine themselves to have attained to a state of sinless perfection. No man that is not blinded to the spirituality of that law which requires supreme, perfect and unabated love, can be insensible to his vast defects. The highest degree of love that we at any time attain, comes immensely short of what we ought to feel, and of what we shall feel when presented faultless before the presence of the divine glory. The only reply that can be made is, that the petition may refer to past sins, and not to present ones. But is it not prescribed along with a prayer for our *daily* bread, and in a prayer which is daily offered?" *

We would meekly join in this confession. To say that we do not sin, is itself a sin. Sure as that we sin daily, do we need forgiveness daily. What we may think to be our sanctities need it, as well as what we call our sins. Our tears need it, our prayers need it, our holiness, our humility, our love. Brothers, there will be times, when, I will not say *although* you are children, but *because* you are—that is, because you have the new perceptive sense that belongs to the new life, you will see in yourselves motives or actions that are tinctured if not stricken through with that which needs forgiveness, there may be moments of fearful revelation when the sudden sight of your sins may have upon you the force of a blow, moments when mercy will be to you the sweetest word in all the Bible, and forgiveness the greatest miracle of mercy.† There

---

* Andrew Fuller's works, vol. vii. p. 306-7.

† Life of John Duncan, LL.D., by Professor David Brown, p. 408. Speaking four days before his death, " of the carnal mind, enmity to God, which the best of men

may also be moments, when, along with an agonized sense of some sin into which, though Christians, you have been surprised, you have a fear that your cry for pardon has not been heard.

A Puritan says, "Howsoever the child of God hath his sinnes fully pardoned at once in God's part on his true repentance; yet he is not able to *receive* pardon at once, but must receive it by little and little, and as it were droppe by droppe; this we may see in David, who had the pardon of his sinne pronounced by Nathan the prophet, 'The Lord also hath put away thy sinne, thou shalt not die' (2 Sam. xii. 13). Yet after that, he penned the fifty-first Psalme wherein he begged mercie and forgiveness most earnestly for that sinne which God had already pardoned, aiming no doubt, at a more comfortable assurance of pardon in his own heart." *

In the ranks of those who profess and call themselves Christians, we find persons who, from two different reasons, are unprepared to join in this petition.

Some, it appears, understand the forgiveness of our rebellion to include, not only the grant of

has at times to fight against," the doctor said, "I never get a sight of it but it produces horror, even bodily sickness," p. 487.

* "The Workes of that Famous and Worthie Minister of Christ in the Vniversity of Cambridge, M. W. Perkins," 1609. Vol III. p. 100.

pardon, but the gift of holiness, and that by one act only of faith, the receiver reaches the perfection of a sinless life—a life which therefore has no further need of forgiveness. A youth lately stood up in a mission room, and addressed a company of four hundred persons to this effect:—

"My friends, I thank God that I can say to-night that I am saved." There was a shout of "Hallelujah!" Then he went on to say, "I go about the town like other folks . . . and they cannot see my heart, but God can see it, and when He looks at my heart He sees that it is whiter than snow. For six months or more, I have not had to ask Him at night to forgive the sins of the day; but I have had every night to thank Him for keeping me from sin. If He can keep me from sin for six months, He can keep me all my life; and if He can keep me, He can keep you—every one of you."

We set down these words of random ignorance, only because they serve to show in bold, blunt plainness, one of those misconceptions and burlesques of the glorious gospel, which seem to be getting common, and which are sometimes reckoned as belonging to the statistics of the Saviour's victories. In giving this prayer, though for the use of all the divine family without an individual exception, he made no provision for a case like this, and was clearly not aware that any single member of it would, while in this world, ever become so free from sin as not to need a daily share in the petition— "Forgive us our trespasses"!

Others being of a different school, contend that we have no need to use a prayer like this, because, although it is quite true that we sin every day, our sins, on to the end of life, are already forgiven. As the ban of the empire is lifted, and our justification in the court of heaven proclaimed, it is impossible that we should have any further forgiveness, and now, instead of prayer for pardon wanted, we have only to offer praise for pardon granted.

"How can a sin be forgiven before it exists? Where do we find a warrant for the idea of pardon for sins before they are lamented or forsaken? Forgiveness invariably presupposes repentance. It is not bestowed *on that account* yet it is inseparably connected with it. As justification includes forgiveness, we may be said to be fully forgiven from the first moment we believe in Christ, but it is in some such way I conceive as we are said to be *glorified*.* The thing is rendered sure by the purpose and promise of God; but as in that case a perseverance to the end is promised and provided for, so is repentance and continual application for mercy through Jesus Christ in this. If it were true

* Rom. viii. 30.

that a believer might not persevere to the end, it would be equally true that he might never be glorified: and if it were possible for him to live in sin and never repent of it, it would be equally possible that he would never be forgiven—but He who has promised that which is ultimate, has provided for everything immediate."*

The act of oblivion which makes our freedom certain is already a fact; but while we are mortal, the pardon itself must be granted perpetually. The treasury of forgiving love is already ours; the payment out of it is only when we ask for it; and this we shall continue to ask, and so continue to have until we have done with sinning. Our salvation is a settled thing; but we shall always be "*receiving* the end of our faith, even the salvation of our souls" until we lift our voices in the shout of eternity—"Salvation to Him that sitteth on the throne and to the Lamb!" All the forgiveness is even now secured, but we have not yet appropriated it all, and the daily prayer "Our Father . . . forgive us our debts," is the daily application for what is already ours, by successive expressions of that faith which grace has made the habit of our existence.

II. It is a prayer for forgiveness in which sin is described as *debt*. That which in the first delivery of the prayer is called debt, in the

* Andrew Fuller.

THE FIFTH PETITION.

second is called sin; much as if the Teacher had said, "it is *sin* that I mean by debt." Indeed, the same doctrine is taught in both passages. What in the first case is asserted, is in the second quite as distinctly implied, for the plea recorded in Luke is, "forgive us . . . as we also forgive every one that is *indebted* to us."

It strikes us that in all the variety and wealth of words used to show the evil qualities and energies of sin, not one is more graphic than this, and not one more mournful.

Even in this earthly life, and with reference to earthly creditors, while still the conscience is sensitive, and the soul alive, scarcely a word in the English language drops on to us with such a deadening blow. It is the horror that holy poverty shrinks from. "I will go into the workhouse rather than go into debt!" Yes, poor old toiler, it would be less shame to be honourably indebted to the laws of your country than to be meanly indebted under false pretences, to any individual.

Debt is the "thing of mystery and fear" that for ever haunts the life even of many a man who keeps up the appearances of wealth. The spectre walks by his side with soundless footfall, sometimes seems to put a freezing hand upon his shoulder, sometimes quickens his steps, sometimes comes round and looks him in the face, suddenly turning it white and wet, sometimes, when he is at home, makes each knock at his door like a sting in his heart, sometimes, as he sits at table, shoots out shadowy fingers to write "on the wall over against him" letters that make him tremble. Debt is agony. Debt stuns the intellect. Debt suffocates. Debt, like a nightmare, benumbs that which it clutches, makes the "right hand forget its cunning, and the tongue cleave to the roof of the mouth!" Debt creates many an evil habit—the habit of staving off by temporary expedients a coming crash; the habit of trusting to chance; the habit of keeping up a desperate composure when on the edge of the worst; habits that gradually harden a man, kill his heart, and blunt the fine chastity of conscience, so that he is still able to run up debts with frightful facility, and to let them grow with soft, noiseless, unsuspected accumulation—debts leading to debts, troubles to troubles, and lies to lies.

Here, speaking of man's relation to God, and his transactions with Him, the Saviour calls our sins our debts. The principle taught is, that sin is not as some would have us think, a weakness, a sickness, an evil in ourselves, and which is only our own affair, but an evil in its aspect towards God. The antecedent sentences suggest, as perhaps they were intended to suggest, what our debts are. Is God our Father? We owe Him loving reverence. Is He in heaven? We owe

THE FIFTH PETITION.

Him a life of heavenly affections and aims. Should we say "Hallowed be Thy name? We owe devotion to His glory. Is it right to say, Thy Kingdom come? We owe Him the tribute of subjects. Is it right to say, Thy will be done? We owe Him, not only the service of the active, but the surrender of the choosing faculties. Is it right to say give us this day our daily bread? We owe Him the worshipping sense of dependence. These things we *owe*. The word "owed" is related to the word "ought," and here is a sad illustration. Payment is not that which *is*, but that which *ought* to be—is still only that which is *owed*. *Duty*, the thing *due*, has not been paid, and out of our own resources we have no means of payment. In the world of commerce, the secret consciousness of being bankrupt is often mastered by reckless levity or forced composure. Sometimes debtors, in despair of paying their debts, afraid to look into their books, or to face the facts of their position, put the whole question away, launch into extravagance, run up tremendous bills, and get into a rate of expenditure beyond their calculations. So does the sinner sometimes act with reference to sin, until God in tender mercy, by His sovereign Spirit, brings him out of his delirium, and makes him cry, "God be merciful to me a sinner!" Sin after conversion is the same thing as sin before it. Sins are always debts.

IV. This is a prayer for *grace*. Forgiveness is an act of grace. It might have been said in the first hour of spiritual awakening: Debtor to God, what do you propose? Compromise? Composition? Plea for patience? Request for time? Engagement to pay by extra service? Atoning for a sinful past by a sinless future? Doing what is over and above your duty?

What, that becomes a man is more than your duty? How can the future cancel the past? Who has told us that keeping clear of debts from this moment would liquidate obligation already contracted? What merchant writes "paid" on a bill simply because his debtor undertakes hereafter to buy only with ready money? Common sense feels insulted.

Our thoughts on the subject all tend to the conclusion with reference to our sins after, as well as before our adoption into the family of God, that there is nothing left for us but to cast ourselves on pure, unmingled clemency; that we have no plea but the plea founded on grace.

V. We advance to the remark that in this prayer for forgiveness, we of course *fall in with the divine plan for its bestowment*. The words here put into the mouth of the suppliant name no plea, show no plan; they suggest nothing, stipulate nothing, but simply ask for the grace, leaving it for the Sovereign to determine the process by which that grace is to come. The first utterers of the prayer knew not, what we all know now, that it comes through him who taught it, and that "we have redemption through his blood, even the forgiveness of sins, according to the riches of his grace." The time had not struck for the outflash of the secret; we know it now, and never separate in our minds the thought of prayer for forgiveness from the thought of the mediating Christ.

"In processes of commerce you see a double page; there is a column on the left hand and a column on the right. The one is called *Charge*, the other *Dis*charge. You observe in settled accounts that although on the side of charge a vast page may be crowded with entries, on the side of discharge there is but a single line; yet accounts at the bottom are equal and balancing. There is a name written underneath the second column; that stands for all the money, and that alone secures the discharge. In the day when God's books are opened, revealing in long lines our heavy debts, Christ's name marked to our account is our discharge."*

In these simple and terse terms was the doctrine once presented. All great ideas of God's ways suffer and dwindle through being distilled through our poor human thoughts and words. Yet such in substance we believe to be a true statement of the way in which grace

* Words of the late Rev. William Arnot, now remembered very imperfectly.

forgives sin. Christ is the representative man. He has so taken upon himself the responsibilities of our debt to God, and so discharged them, that we who live in him and in whom he lives are free!

The humanitarian contends that the doctrine of forgiveness through the suretyship of Christ, really controverts the principle of grace. "Grace gives for nothing; but according to this, God gives for Christ's sake; grace forgives without any payment; God forgives the debtor, because a friend pays for him." So he argues.

Ah! there would be something in this argument if the debtor himself found the friend. But, not only does God himself find the friend, but God *is* the friend—God, in the Son of God, The Supreme Governor of the Universe alone, furnishes the expedient which makes it consistent with the laws of the Universe for Him to forgive the violator of those laws. Interpreting this phrase of the prayer by the facts of the completed gospel, we may fairly take the words, "Our Father, forgive us our debts"— as if they had been written—Our Father, forgive us, for we come to Thee in the name of the Surety whom thou hast appointed, aud who has put our debts away!

VI. *The declaration connected with the prayer.* "Forgive us our debts, as we also forgive our debtors." This declarative sentence impresses us with the certainty that unless we do in the spirit and habit of our lives, forgive those who sin against us, there is no hope for us of divine forgiveness. "Unforgiving, unforgiven." Both versions are faithful to the expression of this meaning, but the new puts it even more emphatically than does the old.

Of course, from what has been already said, it is clear that our forgiveness of sin committed against ourselves, is not the ground and reason of God's forgiveness of our sins against Him. It is not as if we said, "seeing that we forgive those who are indebted to us, *therefore*, O Father! forgive what we owe Thee!" A supposition that would not only attribute to man the meritorious initiative in obtaining his own pardon, but would imply an estimate that brings down to the low level of an insignificant human injury our sins against the Majesty of Heaven.

No! the connection between our forgiveness of each other and God's forgiveness of ourselves, is not one of merit, not one of cause; but one of effect, one of evidence, and so one of unalterable necessity. The law of forgiveness taught by Christ as binding between man and man, like some other laws of his kingdom, is treated as belonging to the class of things called *abstractions*. Men are ready to say — " Very beautiful, doubtless, and very exalted—of course quite right, but impossible to be carried out in actual life." The thought of many an acute practical man about it, would, if cast into language, be something like that lately expressed by a great legislator in the House of Commons, on a proposition that was not deemed to be workable. "I am not friendly, as a general rule, to the assertion in this place of propositions not susceptible of immediate application to practice." "This is a hard saying, who can bear it?" cries the heart. "It is hard indeed, and therefore, likely to be evaded. Why else did Christ make a comment on that petition, passing by the others, when he taught His disciples to pray? And hence it is that injuries are registered in sheets of marble when committed against us, while benefits are written in the sand, ready to be dashed out by the foot of the next that passeth by."* Not only is this the one clause of the prayer to which Christ comes back in the preceptive sentences close following,—but He gives it enforcement by an impressive parable.

"Therefore is the kingdom of heaven likened to a certain king which would make a reckoning with his servants, and when he had begun to reckon, one was brought unto him which owed him ten thousand talents. But forasmuch as he had not wherewith to pay, his lord commanded him to be sold, and his wife and children, and all that he had, and payment to be made.

* Thomas Fuller, Sermons, 1648.

The servant therefore fell down, and worshipped him, saying, lord have mercy on me, and I will pay all. And the lord of that servant being moved with compassion, released him, and forgave him his debt. But that servant went out, and found one of his fellow-servants, which owed him a hundred pence, and he laid hold on him and took him by the throat, saying, Pay me that thou owest. So his fellow-servant fell down and besought him, saying have patience with me, and I will pay thee. And he would not, but went and cast him into prison, till he should pay that which was due. So, when his fellow-servants saw what was done, they were exceedingly sorry, and come and told unto their lord what was done. Then his lord called him unto him, and saith unto him, thou wicked servant, I forgave thee all that debt, because thou besoughtest me; shouldest not thou also have had mercy on thy fellow-servant, even as I had mercy on thee? and his lord was wroth, and delivered him to the tormentors, till he should pay all that was due. So shall also my Heavenly Father do unto you, if ye forgive not everyone his brother from your hearts." *

Perhaps the form of this parable is suggested by the system of blind and oppressive misrule common in eastern countries in olden time. A king of kings would make one of his servants

* Matt. xviii. 23-25.—*Revised Version.*

king under himself of some province in his empire, with the understanding that he might get what taxes he could out of the people, and pay to him, the imperial master, a certain vast amount annually, as a kind of rent. Such a master, here calls such a servant to account for arrears, and the story is used as a vehicle for conveying a lesson on forgiveness. The "certain king," represents God; the "day of reckoning," the day of judgment within us when we stand at the court of conscience, and the Spirit questions us about our sins; the sum of ten thousand talents—the sum owing by the steward—hints at the immensity of what we owe to God. It suggests something not countable, not speakable, not thinkable. "Ten thousand, or a myriad, being the highest number in Greek arithmetical notation; an enormous sum, which, even if the silver talent be designed, amounts to £4,500,000 sterling, but which, if the gold talent be meant, which is far the most likely, then the amount is nearly equal to the annual revenue of the British Empire, that is, equivalent to more than £70,000,000 sterling." *

---

* Substance of a note made by Dr Adam Clarke in 1804. The revenue for the year 1881-2 was reported to be £85,822,000.

How great a sum it was, we may see by comparing it with other sums of which mention is made in Scripture.

THE FIFTH PETITION. 199

I say—you man there! looking so satisfied, feeling so strong—so safe in your standing, so calm in your sense of respectability,—you owe more than seventy millions sterling! unless you pay it, you are lost! This is a figure, but it truthfully expresses a fact. "A duty unfulfilled, is a debt unpaid:" admit this, and you will also admit that your debts to God are more than can be represented by this or any other known symbol. The load is enough to sink a soul, and you are lost!

"Oh no!" cries one, "thank God, no, no! have you not heard? Christ has paid all that debt for me; Christ is my ransom; Christ is my surety; for His sake I have been forgiven all the old life of sin, have been freed from the old sentence of condemnation; the "handwriting that was against me" is crossed out; my place now is not the prison of justice but the palace of the Great King. I am one of His children; I sit at His table; it is true that, child as I am,

---

In the construction of the Tabernacle 29 talents of gold were used (Exod. xxxviii. 24); David prepared for the Temple 3000 talents of gold, and the princes 5000 (1 Chron. xxix. 1-7); the Queen of Sheba presented to Solomon 120 talents (1 Kings x. 10); the King of Assyria laid upon Hezekiah 30 talents of gold (2 Kings xviii. 14); and in the extreme impoverishment to which the land was brought at last, one talent of gold was laid upon it after the death of Josiah, by the King of Egypt (2 Chron. xxxvi. 3).—ARCHBISHOP TRENCH.

I sin every day, and I grieve for this, but I go every day to Him with all His other children, with the petition 'Forgive us our debts,' and so I have forgiveness."

Well, but have you forgiven those who trespass against you? "Yes." Quite sure? "Yes." Have you forgiven and forgotten? Ah no! There is still in some instance a secret reserve. a sleeping grudge. You say "I can forgive, but not forget." Shall God say the same of you? His word is, "I will blot out their transgressions, and remember their iniquities no more."* This is His way of forgiving. If He had said "I will forgive your debts, but I will remember them"; this would have sounded ominously; the forgiveness would not have been thorough, and you would have been ready to cry out in your fear, "Not to forget, is not to forgive."

Chrysostom intimates that many persons in his congregation, when praying, suppressed this clause—"as we forgive our debtors." Do you? Say this after me—"Forgive us, as we forgive our debtors." As the meaning grows upon you, you tremble beneath its weight. Some of you are not able to lift your hand before the Almighty God of truth, and make this declaration, you see also, that prayer for God's pardon so worded, amounts to a prayer that His forgiveness of you may be like your forgiveness of

* Jer. xxxi. 34; Heb. viii. 12.

others—forgiveness, but with reserve, forgiveness of the offence, but with retention of thought about it, therefore conscience keeps you speechless.

Yet if you are not forgiving, there is no warrant for offering prayer that you may be forgiven. It is the Master Himself who has wrought this lesson into the pattern of praying language into which we now look, and in the parable just used as an illustration, he shows the monstrosity of a spirit which a servant who had been forgiven by his king a debt almost too great to be calculated, refuses to forgive his fellow servant one that in comparison with it was almost too small to be named.

Once, when our Lord had been teaching this law of brotherly forgiveness the difficulty of obedience seemed so great to His disciples, and the thought of it so filled them with dismay, that their one instant cry was, "Lord increase our faith"! Let this be our cry, and when in answer to it, faith gets stronger, and we cleave closer to the Crucified One who ever lives to be the medium of our renewed life, we shall have more of His forgiving power. We shall not at once have it to perfection, but we shall go on to perfection in having it. We shall have it in our measure, and as grace grows, that will grow. The Spirit of Him who "creates all things anew," must be within us, to master our vexed and excitable lives, and whenever that Spirit, brooding over the troubled waters of a soul, says, "Let there be forgiveness," there is forgiveness.

IX.

THE SIXTH PETITION.

"And lead us not into temptation."—MATT. vi. 12; LUKE xi. 4. *Authorized Version.*

"And bring us not into temptation."—MATT. vi. 13; LUKE xi. 4. *Revised Version.*

THE Lord's Prayer is for the use of the family while travelling home. This is no easy travelling. A poet, speaking of the modern *"Pilgrim's Progress," reminds us that there can be no railway to the Celestial City—that the journey must still be made in the ancient fashion—made so to speak, *on foot*—made not *for* us, but *by* us. The onward movement is not like that of a carriage, while we are asleep inside it, but must be the result of our own individual volition and exertion. "We *walk*;" and we walk "by faith not by sight." Some of us notice that the shadows begin to lengthen. The day will soon be over. Jesus, our Sun is gone before us, is out of sight, and is already creating the glory

---

See Hawthorne's Allegory of the modern "Pilgrim's Progress" by *rail*.

of the land that we call Heaven. So, we are "stepping westward." Questioned as to this, each one of us might answer—

> "Stepping westward did you say?
> "Stepping westward? Yes alway;
> "With staff and scrip,
> "Wayfaring songs upon our lip,
> "Stepping, stepping to the end."*

"Wayfaring" prayers as well as songs are upon our lip, and this is one—"lead us not into temptation."

I. This is an appeal to our *Leader*.

1. It implies that *our Father is our Leader*. No other leader knows the way. It must be so, for ours is a pilgrimage, not through space, but through time. Whatever else we have seen, we have not seen to-morrow. Whatever maps we have consulted, we have never found a map of the future. No Atlas can help us. The road beyond the moment in which I now plant my foot, is all mist. We know that at some time or other, we may have to wade heavily through black suffocating thoughts that make the "Slough of Despond;" or to toil wearily up the "Hill Difficulty;" or, our spirits quivering with awful touches, to go down into the "Valley of the Shadow of Death," or to be locked in the cell of "Doubting Castle;" or to drink the air and see the beauty of the "Delectable Moun-

* From "Poet's Harvest Home,"—William Bell Scott.

tains." There are lions in the way; and giants for each red cross knight to fight with, but when or where these sceneries may break upon us, or these adventures open, no horoscope can tell. Our Father knows, for "He inhabiteth Eternity," and sees the "end from the beginning." In Him therefore do we place our trust, and to Him do we lift this cry. It does but continue the train of appeal that began in the opening words —" Our Father which art in heaven!" We are not tired by repetition of our familiar hymn—

> Lead Thou me on,
> Keep Thou my feet, I do not ask to see
> The distant scene; one step enough for me.
> I was not ever thus, nor prayed that Thou
>   Should'st lead me on;
> I loved to choose and see my path, but now,
>   Lead Thou me on.
> I loved the garish day, and spite of fears,
>   Pride ruled my will.
> Remember not past years,
> So long Thy power hath blessed me, sure it still
>   Will lead me on,
> O'er moor and fen, o'er crag and torrent, till
>   The night is gone,
> And with the morn, those angel faces smile
> Which I have loved long since,
>   And lost awhile.*

We should make this appeal with a correct understanding of what is here meant by being led. In both instances of its occurrence, the

J. H. Newman.

THE SIXTH PETITION.

latest translators have changed it for the word *bring*. The authorised version in every other instance where the Greek word in question is used, renders it *bring*, and there seems to be no good reason why we should not so translate it here.*

Every one sees the meaning of the word *lead*; we put the same meaning into the word *bring*, only giving it greater strength. "Leading" may mean the gentlest of directive help along the road, but "bringing" is something more energetic. In order to bring, a leader may have sometimes to carry, sometimes to fight, sometimes to clear away obstructions. The pilgrim is his charge, therefore by all needful processes, and in the most effectual way, he fulfils what he undertakes.

This view of our Father's leading is fraught

* μὴ εἰσενέγκῃς. In the authorised version it is translated as follows, in the six other instances of its occurrence in the New Testament.

Luke v. 18, 19. The men who carried the paralytic sought means to "bring him on" to Jesus. The phrase is twice used.

Luke xii. 11. "When they bring you into the synagogues."

Acts xvii. 20. "Thou bringest strange things to our ears."

1 Tim. vi. 7. "We brought nothing into the world."

Hebrews xiii. 11. "The bodies of those beasts whose blood is brought into the sanctuary."

In classical Greek this verb means to bring or carry.

with inspiriting strength. It conveys the idea which holy men by the rivers of Babylon expressed under their favourite phrase, the "Hand of our God is on us." To bring me, He holds me. A family of tourists climbed up certain perilous rocks on the coast of Cornwall; as the father went on first, with his little son, the mother from below, called out to her boy, "have you fast hold of your father"? Then was heard the shrill ring of a voice, answering with perfect sense of safety in its tone—"No, mother, but he has fast hold of me." So is our Father in Heaven leading us by bringing us up through danger, and out of it. Catching sight of certain dangers called temptations, we utter this cry.

2. We make this appeal to our Father with a sense of His *nearness*. We are not saying this to a God who is afar off. Such a God could not at any moment be within hearing, nor could He be leading us. To many God is an almost unimaginable Being, dwelling in the light of infinite splendour, and the reserves of awful solitude, countless millions of miles away, no man having at any time seen His face, or heard his voice, but it is not so with us. We have already learned that just because He is our Father in Heaven, He is everywhere: for He is Lord in Heaven only because He is infinite. The Father leads us through the Son

by the Holy Spirit; and by His Spirit, He is with our spirits. From the necessity of His perfection He is near—near as the hand is to that which it brings, as the air is to that which it fans, as the stream is to that which it laves, as the sun is to the body, diffusing heat through every atom of its frame, and every pulsation of its life. Nay, unspeakably nearer is the intimacy of the Saviour to the saved, for their love to Him is but the indwelling of His own love. Sin is near, sorrow is near, danger is near, Satan is near, death is near, but the soul's Leader is always nearer. This cry is, therefore, not a shout sent up to One who is at a distance; it may be but a thought that scarcely emerges from silence, a mere movement of the soul to Him who is nearer than near; and, when from the agony of my panic, I can find no voice, He who is leading me is so close to me, that He hears the trembling of the unspoken prayer, "Bring us not into temptation."

II. This petition comes from the fear that when in answer to our last petition, our sins are forgiven, *we shall be tempted to sin again.* We have just asked for forgiveness, because, although heaven born and heaven bound, we are always failing to pay what our spirits owe; are always like Christ's first disciples, even while going with Him up to Jerusalem, hurting His love by a spirit contrary to His own; are always needing to renew our entreaty for pardon.

You therefore see the connection betweeu what we now are saying, and what has just been said. This connection is suggested by the introductory use of the word "and." Now, as in the last instance in which the particle has this peculiar place—it links two petitions together, so that the spirit of the first still runs on into the second. If the hurry of our joys at the answer to our prayer "forgive us our debts," should make us forget to add, "lead us not into temptation," the weight of debt may be scarcely lifted, before we are in debt again. That sentence is therefore followed up by this. Having pardon for the past, we want grace for the future, and so have within us the longing which made an ancient suppliant say—"Thou hast delivered my soul from death; will not Thou deliver my feet from falling, that I may walk before God in the light of the living?"*

We find that in the Bible, the word temptation is used with two different meanings. Sometimes it simply means to *try;* sometimes to *entice;* the purpose in the one case being good, in the other—evil.

When, on the one hand, we read that "God did tempt Abraham," we understand the term

* Psalm lvi. 13.

as meaning that He tried him as the pruner tries the tree, the refiner the silver, as the strong strain or dead weight tests the efficiency of that which has hard work to do.

When, on the other hand, we read that "Satan did tempt David," we understand that he enticed him to sin. Granted, that all temptation includes trial—that even a temptation plied by Satan is often used by Satan's Master, and over-ruled to be a Divine instrument for the invigoration of our faith—that what was meant for evil is transmuted into good, and that the ultimate issue defeats the primary design; still, temptation is meant by the evil one to work nothing but evil, and it is against this kind of temptation that we now pray. We tremble at the thought of sin: and pray to our Leader that we may not be led into it.

III. We thus pray, because we know that *our path abounds with instruments and occasions of temptation.*

These would not be so certainly dangerous, if they all had open advertisement—if danger-signals hung out near all danger—if everything that had in it the nature of hell made itself visible by the light of its own hell-fire—if every snare had the word " Temptation " written on it, by the hand of mystery that wrote on the palace wall of Babylon, you would keep out of its way; "for in vain is the snare spread in the sight of any bird." You would not bathe in brightest waters while seeing sharks play there; you would catch up no basket of flowers like Cleopatra's if you saw the asp lifting its head from below, for only the lunatic will " dally with the crested worm." Life is not in love with death ; and the instincts of holiness would make the Christian shun a sin when known to be a sin, even without the warning, "avoid it, pass not by it, turn from it and pass away." But it is not so. The sin that is near us constantly hides itself under a false colour and a wrong name.

We may be led into temptation, when *in business*. Business is not in itself a sin. It is not a sin to make the most of the earth, to get the most out of it, to make it answer, to turn it into value, and to do that with it which creates wealth. The commandment to "dress and keep" the garden in which God has set man, so as to "replenish and subdue the earth," was given before the fall, and is still binding on us; but in the world as it now is, who does not know that while in pursuance of this lawful end, we may be led into something that is unlawful? When a thing that is in itself only subsidiary, is interesting, there is a tendency to take too keen an interest in it. Dealing with earthly things, we may be too eager to gain them, too grasping to keep them, and too sorrowful to let them go.

We may be mastered by the law of assimilation, and so become like the elements that we work in. "Bury a man in earth," says the shrewd Owen Feltham, "and he himself will soon be earth."

We may be led into temptation *by the habits of society*. Let me try to make my meaning plain by a parable.*

Sometime after the last of the Apostles died, there lived at Ephesus a thriving man of business named Marcus, who was an elder of the Church. His wife, though, like himself, an accredited member of the church, was scarcely reclaimed from the prevailing heathenism, and still cherished with sentimental interest, though not with belief, the old poetic stories of Apollo and Venus, Jove and Diana.

Their children, as the children of persons rising in life, were sent to schools suited to the rich or the risen class, and where it was thought a sign of respectability to honour "the fair humanities of old religion." Naturally, the associates of these children, as they grew older, were the fashionable heathen. They entreated and coaxed their parents in one thing after another to conform to heathen usages. "Why should we be singular?" it was said, "Why should we not be at feasts where, just for mere form's sake, libations

---

* This is suggested by a story read long ago, though I fail to remember the thread of it, nor can I say where it is given.

are made to Apollo, so long as we do not believe in Apollo? Why should we refuse meats consecrated to the heathen gods, when every one knows that this consecration means nothing? How are we to reclaim the heathen, if we never mingle with them? and besides, did not our Master sit with publicans and sinners?"

Marcus was a man courteously inclined, easily entreated, happy to see others happy, especially sympathetic with the happiness of youth; and just now, on the principle "that extremes beget extremes," was tempted to the extreme of laxity because some Christians had gone to the extreme of stringency — making as he justly thought, religion appear to the young, less like a divine principle than a hardy, narrow, censorious prejudice. So, afraid to create a prejudice in young minds against religion, gradually, but uneasily, the good Marcus gave way.

Gradually, you saw his children at heathen festive meetings held at their friends' houses. "Why not! The heathen should never have ground for saying that Christians are morose." Gradually, toiler though he was, his own house would become the scene of a sumptuous entertainment, where, between the toil of yesterday and the toil of to-morrow, hot, exhausted crowds, in hot exhausted air, would be in mazy motion most of the night. "Why not? Entertainments of this kind," it would be said, "are absolutely necessary to maintain our position, and if we accept them, we must return them." Gradually you saw about his walls, silver or marble statuettes of Jupiter or Venus. "Why not? They are not for worship, of course; they are placed there simply in compliance with the general usage of good society." Gradually in the course of these evening entertainments, exquisite perfumes from censers richly wrought, would be waved before these images. "Why not? It is always done; nobody means anything by it; and as for the statuette, we know that an idol is nothing in the world."

At last, fellow Christians would venture on remonstrance. Then the young people in the family of Marcus would fire up, and answer grandly—"You tell us that we are in danger. We tell you that we know when to stop. You tell us that we distress the consciences of persons in the church, who keep to the simplicity of the old faith, and check the decision of converts. We beg to reply, that we glory in everything broad, and scornfully repudiate everything narrow. The meanest of all influences over conduct, is that which comes from the thought of what others may think. Others may think it religion to shut themselves up and read the old gospel manuscripts; we stand up for our own rights; and, whatever others do, as for us, and our house, we will please ourselves." So by degrees, they were led into temptation, and at length it became impossible to tell from any social signs, whether these advanced Christians were servants of Jesus or of Jupiter. Let us, as far as it is needful, apply the principle thus suggested, to the circumstances of our own day.

We may be led into temptation by *retiring from the world.* It must be plain to every one who forms a fair estimate of men as they are, that the great majority of them regard Christian principles as expounded in the New Testament, with dead indifference or sarcastic hostility. The *many* are of the world; the *few* are not of it. So patent is this fact, and so patent has it ever been, that according to the supreme book, the term "world," marking the ungodly, is the term that also represents the idea of society in general; obviously importing, that, in the judgment of inspiration, the ungodly form the mass of mankind. This is an alarming consideration, for it implies that if we are thorough-going Christians, we have to hold our ground or make our way against an opposing mass. Surely that which has at once mass and momentum, weight and velocity, must carry all before it! It has often been thought therefore, that there is no safety for those who are "not of the world" but by getting out of its way.

If we attempt this by retirement into some scene of quiet happiness, we may there meet with new temptations. In the middle ages, when it was a common article of belief that the garden of Eden, though a holy secret, guarded by angels, still flowered in all its glory in some Eastern land, many a terrified soul in wicked city or monastic cell, would doubtless dream of the blessedness there would be in finding the spot, and dwelling there guarded from Satanic spells.

Yet, Paradise was the scene of the fall, and there it was that man was first led into temptation. Be sure that if we could find or make some earthly Paradise of our own, where we might hear "the voice of the Lord God walking in the trees of the garden," where "the world forgetting and the world forgot," holy love would tremble into tenderness, thought into flame, and where there would be no outward interruptions to prayers, even there, a tempting spirit would find us.

If, on the other hand, we fled into a wilderness, we should still be followed. In the same old times at which we have just glanced, devotion has often sped in alarm from the world into the wilderness. The devotee has many a day made his escape to some stern solitude, where, a cave his house, a litter of leaves his bed, roots his food, his drink the crystal spring— he has tried to crucify every natural inclination, to strain all humanity out of his body, and to steep his soul in ghastly meditations, that thus he might keep out Satan. But old legends testify that on such lives Hell has often spent its utmost fury, and that in such conditions, poor souls have suffered most from the poison of idle thought or polluting fancy.

Though the first Adam was tempted in a garden, the second was tempted in a wilderness. There it was, that through forty days, with no rich fruits to stay the sting of hunger, no clear stream rippling over golden sands to slake his thirst, no shelter from the fiery day or the freezing night, and where—beauty banished, grim desolation sat enthroned, He who afterwards died for us, was tempted, and the wilderness was the memorable field in which man's great representative fought with man's great foe. After this, let no follower of His hope to escape "the fiery darts of the wicked one," by living in any wilderness of self-inflicted poverty or pain. The principle of seeking retirement from the world of temptation, either in some kind of Eden or in some kind of wilderness is always being tried in some form or other, and always fails.

We may be led into temptation even when we feel most secure from it *by communion with God*. When was Christ himself tempted? Bishop Hall says, "No sooner has Christ come out of the waters of baptism, than he comes into the fire of temptation. No sooner does the Spirit come in the form of a dove, than he is 'led by the Spirit into the wilderness.' No sooner doth God say 'this is my beloved Son in whom I am well pleased,' than Satan darts the suggestion of doubt, '*if* Thou be the Son of God.'" We have in Christ's experience a rehearsal of what is likely to be our own. It is a specimen of what is common in the tempter's strategy. After a season of profit and privilege, you may expect to be caught in some artifice or challenged to some deadly fight. The robber of the soul waits for the moment when the soul, being most happy, is least cautious, and has most to lose. "It is the man bringing his dividend from the banker's door who has most cause to dread the pilferer's hand."*

IV. It implies *a sense of our own temptableness*. When angels have been sent to this world on errands of wrath or love they have moved sinless through an atmosphere of sin, and amidst its worst infections, they could no more be infected than snow flakes could catch fire, or sunbeams take pollution. But even before it was vitiated, mere humanity was in itself temptable. The perfect Son of Man was in "all points tempted as we are." It was a real temptation that He suffered. His victory mplies this, for there could have been no victory

* Cardiphonia.

in an imaginary conflict with an imaginary foe. At least, there is always in our nature a certain weakness to which the tempter can make his appeal. Of this weakness a thoughtful writer remarks, " There lies deep down in every man's nature an unsuspected weakness to which temptation may make a sudden appeal with success, and he may do some wicked thing in consequence unlike his general character altogether. The tempter may come, and the tempter does come in—to storm and command the very citadel of his soul. In that instant the man is not himself, but another. He is himself in so far as that he himself is responsible. He is *not* himself, but another, and that other the evil one, in so far as that the evil one is for the moment master in that house of clay, and the man himself seems to be living, breathing, thinking, doing by substitution. It is then that he acts as he never acted before, and never will God helping him, again. It is then the great contradiction takes place. He will do that to which his nature has most instinctive repulsion, and which will rob his after life of all tranquillity."*

Besides natural weakness, we have severally and constitutionally, a bias in the direction of some particular sin. "Every man is tempted when he is drawn by his own lust and enticed."†
There are moments when he will feel drawn,

* The Rev. Page Roberts in " Law and God."
† James i. 14.

as a vehicle is drawn—when perhaps some propensity will pull him, as a horse pulls towards its own stable, where it gets what it likes. This peril is in his own being. He may go away out of the circle of most urgent instruments and occasions of temptation, but he can never go away from himself. Every one has a soul, and every one has a body. Once a disciple might have said, "I at least, am safe; I have seen the Lord; I am a spiritual man; I am inspired." Let it, however, be remembered that it was to disciples who could each say this that the alarming charge was given, "Take heed to yourselves, lest at any time your hearts be overcharged with surfeiting and drunkenness, and cares of this life."* What Christ said to his own immediate followers, He says with seven-fold emphasis to us—"Take heed to *yourselves!*"

Preaching to Wiltshire ploughmen, Augustus Hare says that each man must shun things that tempt him to the sin he himself most likes, and must remember that these things, though perhaps no snare to another man, when that other man most likes some other kind of sin—may be to himself full of deadly danger.

"What may be no temptation to another man, may, from some weakness of character or dis-

* Luke xxi., 34.

position, be a crafty snare to me. Therefore it becomes me to avoid it. If you had a ditch to cross on your way to work, and it was so broad that you could not leap over it, after trying and tumbling once or twice perhaps, you would go round by the bridge. It would be no reason to you that neighbour such a one could leap it. You would say, He is welcome to leap it then; but I can only leap *into* it: I have tried twice already: twice have I only wetted myself and dirtied my clothes: so I will not run the risk again! The safe way over the bridge is good enough for me.

In like manner, if by frequenting such a place, or such a company, you have fallen once or twice into sin, listen not to the tempter when he bids you try again. Say within yourself: I have tried too often. I will run no further risk of hurting and dirtying my soul. Christ has cleansed it with His blood; it is too precious a thing to be polluted." *

Let us apply the principle thus given out with such homely force to certain things which in our day are increasingly connected with the question of temptation. To theatricals, or to any other mode of popular amusements. Is it true that all these things are in their essence wrong? Who says they are? Is it true that certain

* The Alton Sermons, by Augustus W. Hare. 1874, pp. 479, 480.

institutions for amusement, look to their support from the majority, must therefore please the taste of the majority, that majority having no taste for holiness? Is it true that their proprietors must meet the market or lose their money? Is it true in consequence, that they are likely to hinder rather than help the highest life? Such questions claim thoughtful and prayerful consideration, but set them aside at present, for a question that practically comes first—and that is, what will be the probable effect of such recreations on yourself as a Christian? Whatever dissipates the force or chills down the fervour of your devotional life; whatever weakens your working life, your teaching life, or your missionary life; whatever indisposes you to read your Bible, whatever prevents you from joyfully inhaling the spirit of the Scriptures as a hot and weary man drinks the air of the spring morning; whatever makes infrequent the moments of Divine visitation and exalted spirituality, the thoughts of clear criteria and the flashes of revealing light by which you better understand yourself, and better understand your Saviour; whatever makes the thought of Christ fall like a cold shadow on the sunshine of your joy; whatever you would rather not try to thank God for, or to ask a blessing on; whatever brings a chilling change from bright and blissful faith to dull despondency, or from spiritual manhood to second infancy; whatever is the cause of failing trust, or freezing love, or slackened service—however lawful it may be to another man, is not lawful for you. Recreation is lawful. Yes, it is lawful as the sparkling dew, lawful as the spring, lawful as the flowers—but says Richard Baxter, "there is no mirth like the mirth of believers," and any particular mode of recreation that in my own experience, still to borrow his words, "impairs the mirth which faith doth bring from the precious blood of Christ, and from the promises of the Word, and from experiences of mercy, and from fore-apprehensions of everlasting blessedness," is no recreation for me.

It would be simply rational for any man to say, When I know, and I ought to know, what are my own sinful propensities, I would not of my own will be led within the range of what might stir them into activity. There is in old Arabic fable, the story of a great rock that was a great magnet, drawing ships, so that they were dashed into splinters on it. If I have been magnetized by a certain sin, I would not be led near the loadstone that might draw me into destruction by its malignant potency. If I carry in me, the gunpowder of some slumbering badness, I would not be led where sparks are flying. If I am "Little Faith" bearing precious jewels, I would not be led through "Dead Man's Lane," where robbers lurk. If I am short-sighted, I would not be led into "the land of pits." If I am timid, and fear "the power of the dog,"* I would not be led near his chain, but far as may be beyond the reach of his spring. If I am constitutionally passionate, I would not be led into the company of those who are likely to put me into a passion; if sceptical, I would not give myself to the study of sceptical books; if I am vain, I would not be led through "Vanity Fair;" if I am in danger from sympathy with any one particular sin, I would avoid the familiar thoughts that slope the way to it, as I would keep away from the top of the smooth granite slope that borders the black, deep well. I would not tempt the tempter, by bringing what is so temptable directly under his power, and would never cease to cry to our Father, "Lead us not into temptation."

V. By this petition, we mean *that we have no will to go into temptation unless it be the will of God to lead us into it.*

* Psalm xxii. 20. "I remember to have read a story of one Gunno, king of the Danes, that having overcome a people, he set a dog over them to be their governour: that is, he would have his commands to go out under the name of the dog, and they should be under the government of the dog; this he did in disdain and indignation against those people he overcame. Much more debasement is it for a soul to be under command of the devil."—*Jeremiah Burroughs.*

THE SIXTH PETITION. 225

We have heard of a man who had unlawful possession of another man's estate, through concealing the knowledge of the former owner's last will, which had unexpectedly to him left it away to some one else. He was tempted to destroy it, but had not quite made up his mind to do so. One night he fought his conscience down, kept his qualms under, and tried to sleep. He even repeated the Lord's Prayer to himself when under the sheets; struggling, however, as he did so, not to think about the petition, "Lead us not into temptation." Do we know that state of mind?

If in uttering these words, we dare not weigh their meaning, if we are in the mood of yielding to some evil besetment, and have some dormant intention which we would rather not wake up to look at—then, while in the very act of speaking to the Almighty God of truth, we say one thing and mean another, and, however unconsciously, utter words of worship in the spirit of profanity.

It is essential to the reality of this, as of the connectional petitions, that before coming to it, we should pray, "Thy will be done." The larger petition governs the smaller. It may seem like inconsistency first to say, "Lead us into temptation if it be Thy will;" then to say, "Lead us *not* into it"—but there is no inconsistency. It is only akin to the Saviour's prayer, when He went into Gethsemane, saying with shrinking and tremulous dread, "Father, if it be possible, let this cup pass from me, nevertheless, not my will, but Thine be done." The innocent instincts of His appropriated nature shuddered at the cup, but were not allowed to keep Him from drinking it, when the Father put it into His hand. The spirit that offers this petition in the model prayer, is still a spirit that will, if commanded, make us "count it all joy when we fall into manifold temptations," while the Lord is there. Jesus was led up into "the wilderness to be tempted of the devil." Led like Him, we will venture to go like Him, into that which would be in itself pain the most exquisite, and peril the most extreme. That which is the leading power, will be the sustaining power. He who guides, will hold. While you say, my soul abhors this place, you will be able to add, but my God brought me into it, it is therefore the pathway of promise, the thoroughfare to the land of triumph. The trial of your faith will be turned into a proof of your sonship, for "as many as are led by the spirit of God, they are the sons of God."

It is said of Jesus whose steps we are to tread in, that "He being *full* of the Holy Ghost, returned from Jordan, and was led by the Spirit into the wilderness." *

---

* It is said (Matt. iv. 1), that "He was led up," ($ανήχθη$) and (Luke iv. 1) that " He was led ($ήγετο$) by the Spirit

This strikes us as a strong contrast to the reckless rush and flippant levity with which men often plunge into dangers so great that it would need a miracle to bring them out unscathed. "Be ye filled with the Spirit," is the Divine law for us. Can we, when thus filled, go from our own preferences into the haunts of sin? Our Father never sends His children into them on any needful errand, or for any wise discipline, without this preparation. "He never," says an old writer, "suffers His castles to be besieged till they be provisioned." With this equipment, it may be His will that we should enter fields where we have to face the full array of evil, and brave the full blast of storms. But however charged with the Spirit's influence, we shall not step into a post of great moral hazard without clear orders. Once, while William of Orange was laying siege to a town on the Continent, an officer with a message ventured to go to the spot where he was in the act of directing the operation of his gunners. When the message was delivered, and the answer to it received, he

into the wilderness to be tempted of the devil." The word means that going into the wilderness was His own act, though not of his own desire, but with a will that consented to the will of the Father. The word "bring" ($εισενέγης$) in our prayer points to the act of God in taking us into temptation, and in this case, our consent of will takes the form of resignation rather than of active obedience still lingered. "Sir," said the prince, "do you know that every moment you stand here is at the risk of your life?" "I run no more risk," replied the gentleman, "than your highness." "Yes," said the prince, "but my duty brings me here, and yours does not." In a few minutes a cannon-ball struck the officer dead. While only led by our own inclination into a risk, we have no divine guarantee of protection. Led and filled by God Himself, our souls are safe anywhere. Not only so, but temptations will be made subservient to the highest purposes of profit to man and glory to God. Overcome, they will keep us closer to Him who is leading us, make us lowlier God-ward, and more sympathetic man-ward. Victors who have been tempted are the wisest teachers, and the strongest helpers of those who are tempted now. Still, though the result may be so gracious, the process is so trying that it is right to say, "Father, if it be possible, spare me. It is not my own choice to go, if it be Thy will lead me into some other path, but if it be Thy will to lead me in this I will go. I will go in the strength of the Lord God, making mention of Thy righteousness and that only."

X.

THE SEVENTH PETITION.

"But deliver us from evil." MATT vi 13; LUKE xi 4.—
Authorized Version.

"But deliver us from the evil one." MATT. vi 13—
Revised Version.

Omitted from the Gospel by Luke.

WE glory in our old English Bible. The knowledge of eternal life first reached us through its pages; it is our counsellor; it has been our solace in many a trouble; and apart from its intrinsic preciousness as a divine revelation, its mere style is matchless. The longer we live, the more do we feel its serene grace, its moving music, and its grand, antique simplicity.

We have, however, no share in the sentiment of those who seem to think that any attempt to revise this translation, is to take a liberty with things sacred. The element of sacredness belongs to the Word, not to this or that translation of it. The first is the gift of God, and as such, is perfect; the second is the work of man, and partakes of man's imperfection. When God's flour is ground in man's mill, "it is apt

to get mingled with grit from the mill-stone," *
and we are always glad when this can be cleared
out again. Perfection admits of no improve-
ment, but scholarship is in its nature a progressive thing; and in no department has it
been more remarkably progressive than in this.
When Erasmus published his Greek Testament
in 1516,† he had access to only six MSS. ‡
Instead of six, we have now more than sixteen
hundred. Very ancient versions in other
languages have also been found out within this
period of 365 years; still further helping to
settle the true text. During the same time
there has been much research into the folios of
the Fathers, where are Biblical quotations so
numerous that if the sacred MSS. had perished,
most of the Greek Testament might have been
recovered from these authorities alone. There
has been a growing knowledge of materials, and
a growing education of power to estimate their

* Bengel.

† The New Testament in the Complutensian Polyglot
though printed in 1514, was not published till 1522.

‡ Five of these are now in the public library of Basle,
and one is in that of the Prince of Oettingen-Wallerstein.

It is said that two of these MSS. he only used for
occasional reference. For the gospels, he only had what
Dr Scrivener calls "an inferior manuscript," of the
fifteenth century; for the Apocalypse, a mutilated manuscript of the twelfth century. For the Acts and Epistles
he had a manuscript of the thirteenth century.

value. The result is, that "the critical apparatus of the New Testament has increased a hundred-fold." We who are honestly concerned, first to know what God really says, next to know what He really means, eagerly avail ourselves of these helps; and feel in particular immeasurably indebted to the twenty-eight scholars, who, after ten years of patient labour, have given us the last Revised Version of the New Testament.

Still, some of us would have been glad if a few of the alterations given in the text, had only been placed in the margin; and glad especially if this had been done here. The evil *person*, and the evil *thing* are both expressed in the Greek Testament by the adjective with the article. In the nominative and accusative cases, the difference in the ending leaves no doubt as to which is meant; but the masculine and neuter of genitive and dative are alike. In this instance, the original words are only these two—"the evil," and we are unable at present to see just cause for adding a third, so as to read "the evil *one*." The change from the abstract to the personal is not imperative from the termination of the Greek word which in this petition we have been accustomed to render "evil;" nor does the word for "deliver" require it, nor the preposition for "from." In the Revised Version of 2 Tim. iv. 18. we read, "the Lord will deliver me from every evil work, and will save me unto His heavenly kingdom;" yet the verb, the preposition, and the adjective for "evil," are all the same as in the Lord's Prayer. In the Septuagint, the phrase is constantly employed in the abstract, never in the personal sense. It is said, indeed, that the Greek Fathers use it in the latter sense, but on the other hand, it might be contended that the only expositors thus quoted, lived two hundred years after the Apostles; and the meaning of the word should, we think, be settled not by the usage of their day, but by that of the day when Christ uttered it, if that could be ascertained.* Upon the whole, the change made by the revisers expresses but a supposed probability, and not an ascertained or ascertainable fact. It is no presumption to say this, for the most competent scholars are divided in opinion about the matter.† Feeling must not

* Origen tells us in his treatise *De Oratione*, that the words ἀλλὰ ῥῦσαι ἡμᾶς ἀπὸ τοῦ πονηροῦ are not a part of the prayer as found in the gospel of Luke. We believe that no reference is to be found to this in the writings of any Greek Father before his time. He died about A.D. 254.

† Among the critical and textual expositors who are in favour of adopting as the reading, "The evil one," are Doddridge, Adam Clarke, Olshausen, Mayer, Godet, Keim, Ebrard, Samuel Davidson, Plumptre, Wordsworth, Ellicott. Among those who decide for "the evil," Tyndale, the Geneva Version, Isaac Barrow, Weiss, Keil, Ewald, Tholuck, Bleek, Lange, Stier, Mansel, Canon Cook, and Alford

Alford thinks that the general meaning of the two closing petitions is this. "Bring us not into conflict with colour judgment. Only the laws of language can settle what is only a question of language. But this is a question which these laws alone are not competent to settle. Mere grammar would allow of either translation. The connection, together with appearances of probability must help us to decide as to which of the two is most likely to be right, and thus ruled, we are inclined still to vote for the common reading. We are convinced of its natural force and reasonableness. It is exactly what might have been expected; it accords with the ideal of a prayer with this comprehensive scope, and this view to universal use. The prayer has in it no personal term excepting the invocation, and it would indeed have been surprising to find it end with this appeal against a personal enemy; it would have been stranger still to find that all through we had been travelling up to this climax, that we should end in a cry for deliver-

evil, but rather deliver (rid) us from it altogether." He regards the last petition "as expressing the deep desire of all Christian hearts to be delivered from *all evil* (for τοῦ πονηροῦ is here certainly neuter; the introduction of the mention of 'the evil one' would here be quite incongruous and even absurd), these words form a seventh and most affecting petition, reaching far beyond the last. They are the expression of the yearning for redemption of the sons of God (Rom. viii., 23), and so are fitly placed at the end of the prayer, and as the sum and substance of the personal petitions"

ance from one solitary wicked spirit, and that the very last word of the Lord's Prayer should be the one that stands for the devil. Jesus, we think, was unlikely to make His last word one of terror on account of his conquered and humiliated foe.

I. We shall try to identify "the evil" here named. The words here descriptive of what we seek to be delivered from, are only these—"the evil." Our Authorised Version reads "*evil*" simply; but in the original there is the article, Take notice also that this word "evil" is, as grammarians say, in the singular case. Christ names "the evil." He seems to score the word, and to speak it in capitals: "THE EVIL!" He who sees all things, past, present and to come, in all their deep meanings, vast connections and mystic mighty spells; and Who knows the nature and history of all evils in the darkness and under the sun, here separates and singles out one thing from all the rest, and calls it *the evil*. As if amidst the millions, this is the only one worth a notice or a name, amidst all the present perils of our being, this one stands out in such dread, lurid, lone pre-eminence, that all the rest are nothing to it. It is the one to fear, the one to fight with, the one to be held in perpetual abhorrence, and against which we are to make perpetual prayer. It is the one arch mischief and master sorrow of humanity, for deliverance from whose vassalage we should be

ready to part with all else that we most care for. "If thy right eye offend thee, pluck it out, and cast it from thee; for it is profitable for thee that one of thy members should perish, and not that thy whole body should be cast into hell. And if thy right hand offend thee, cut it off, and cast it from thee; for it is profitable for thee that one of thy members should perish, and not that thy whole body should be cast into hell."*
"The evil." It is a terrific phrase! Like an alarm sounded over a congregation of sleeping spirits, it should ring them up, make them all broad awake in a moment, and listen as if they had never listened before! We say that the evil is *Sin*. What else can it be?

Not *the world*. Language, sometimes in books, sometimes "floating on the lips of the wise," gives the impression that some disciples think that by "the evil" Christ means the world. What world? The world which at the call of God, sprang beautiful and perfect from the maze of primitive confusion? The world which at the beginning, He six times over pronounced to be very good? The world out of whose seeds, roots and hidden forces, grow into lovely and wonderful expression, the thoughts of God Almighty? The world out of whose forms prophets drew their imageries, and the gospel its types? Do they mean the world

* Matthew v. 29, 30.

of social existence? Many think so. They would indeed disclaim the old ascetic doctrine that we have lately hinted at. They love the landscapes and the seasons, because they are God's handiwork, and study natural life, architecture, and history with delight, because these aid them in marking the evolutions of the all pervading Mind; but they turn away from the foci of human life, and exclaim with Cowper, "God made the country, but man made the town."

No! God made the town as well as the country. "He who gave to the bee or the bird or the beaver instincts for their own wonderful works and ways, has also furnished the human mind with those faculties and tendencies which, under favouring circumstances, develope in railways and palaces as surely as the beaver-mind developes in moles and embankments, or as the bee-mind developes in combs and hexagons. The skill is Jehovah's; in every fair work of skill, every fine result of calculation, and more especially in everything that helps happy development of human life, you ought to recognise the divine perfections as their ultimate origin no less than if you read on every object 'Holiness to the Lord.' In art, science, machinery, intellectual achievement, an enlightened disciple may discern the manifestations of that mind which is 'wonderful in counsel, excellent in working,' and so far as skill, adaptation and elegance are involved, will hail the Eternal Builder Himself as the Maker of the town."

In the prayer which sums up His intercession for all disciples, our High Priest draws a distinction between the world and the evil in it. "I pray not that Thou shouldest take them out of the world, but that Thou shouldest keep them from the evil."

If you want to know what this evil* is, ask one who, more than any other of those immortals, known as inspired men, was most at home in divine thoughts, and he will say, "Ye have overcome the evil one. Love not the world, neither the things that are in the world. If any man love the world, the love of the Father is not in him. For all that is in the world, the lust of the flesh, and the lust of the eye, and the vain glory of life, is not of the Father, but is of the world.".

Affliction is not "*the* evil." It would be another thing to say it is not *an* evil. We call that ancient, not a stoic merely, but a mono-

---

* John xvii. 15. Here, according to the Revised Version, we are to read "the evil one," but as in the Lord's Prayer the meaning of ὁ πονηρός has to be determined solely by the requirements of the context, and these appear to me to decide for the old reading rather than for the new. We are quite unable to think that our Lord, in words spoken when leaving the world, prayed so emphatically that His disciples might be kept from him whom He had already conquered, and whom He had seen "fall like lightning from Heaven." By the evil He must have meant sin.

maniac, who cried when in mortal agony—"Oh pain, pain, 'tis to no purpose this, thou shalt never make me confess that thou art an evil." We own pain to be an evil, poverty an evil, slander an evil, every kind of sorrow an evil. And when all these seem to burst upon a man in one driving storm, he may naturally cry "Innumerable evils have compassed me about." "From lightning and tempest; from plague, pestilence, and famine; from battle and murder, and from sudden death, good Lord deliver us." This language of the Litany is the dictate of nature, and has the sanction of grace; but we must only use it in continuance of the secret prayer, "Thy will be done." For lightning and tempest, plague, pestilence and famine, and all other evils, belong to the system in which "we know that all things work together for good to them that love God, to them who are the called according to His purpose." The plan of the divine Disciplinarian is not to take us out of troubles, but to make troubles our teachers. Even worldly wisdom can see that it is often a grander thing to strengthen the back than to lighten the burden on it; to bring out the steel of the arm than to lessen the work it has to do; to make a ship fit for a hurricane than to keep it for ever in a dead sea. Under the rule of the spirit, such ends do many of these evils work, and we must have a care how we pray to be delivered from them, lest, such prayers being answered, deliverance should itself be an evil.

A "tribulum" is a flail;* "tribulation" is only the process of using it, but the corn is brought under that process for good and not for evil. Hear the song of a Puritan poet:—

> "Till from the straw the flail the corn doth beat
> Until the chaff be purged from the wheat,
> Yea, till the mill the grains in pieces tear,
> The richness of the flour will scarce appear;
> So, till men's persons great afflictions touch,
> If worth be *found* their worth is not so much,
> Because like wheat in straw they have not yet
> That value which in threshing they may get.
> Until the bruising flail of God's corrections
> Have threshed out of us our vain affections;
> Till these corruptions which do misbecome us
> Are by Thy sacred spirit winnowed from us;
> Until from us the straw of worldly treasures—
> Till all the dusty chaff of empty pleasures—
> Yea, till his flail upon us He doth lay
> To thresh the husk of this our flesh away,
> And leave the soul uncovered; nay, yet more,
> Till God shall make our very spirit poor,
> We shall not up to highest wealth aspire;
> But then we shall; and that is my desire." †

Only as you call a flail evil, that separates the grain from the chaff; a wheel evil that grinds jewels to burn in a crown; a knife evil

* Virg Geor. I., 164.
† George Wither.

that prunes a tree; a tree evil that bears good fruit; a plough evil whose colter crashes through the hard soil, opens it to the chemistry of nature, and makes it a soft, porous, receptive seed-plot for the harvest; the medicine evil that brings back the colour of health to the white face, and the flash of gladness to the dim eye; the hand evil that snatches back a heedless child from the nest of the serpent, or the lip of the river, just in time to save its life—only in this qualified sense can you call an affliction an evil. Out of our greatest sorrows grow our greatest joys. The worst of all these is not evil itself; not all these together could make what is here set down as "the evil."

It is not *death*. With soft step and by mysterious ways, the last enemy may approach us. We may come slowly into his power without knowing it. Indeed, the captive may not for a long time be aware that it is he who is holding him. He may say, "What is this freezing, malignant presence? This pain, how is it to end? Tell me, can this be death? Into what unknown land is this fearful thing carrying me?"

A little blind child, close clasped up against her father, was carried by him into a room in a strange house. One who was in the room, stepped quietly up, unclasped his arms, and without saying a word, or making a sign, lifted

THE SEVENTH PETITION.

the child away. "You seem not to be much frightened," said the father; "do you know who has you?" "No," she said, "but I am not afraid, for I know you know who has me."*
Like that little child, though in the grasp of mystery, while I am near my Father, "I will trust, and not be afraid."

To those, indeed, who are not ready, it is a horror. They only know death as life's great foe, and have no antidote to its natural repellency. Fixing our thoughts on certain refusers of Christ, we say, " O God, spare them! Let them not see the face of Death yet! Spare them, 'that they may gather strength, before they go hence, and are no more seen!' Spare them awhile, though to suffer; spare them that if even brought by the discipline of sorrow they may come to Thee, that they may have life!"

Once, in the days of the Scottish Covenanters, when a congregation met in a great green cup of wild heather, while watchers were posted on peaks of the round rim above; suddenly an alarm was given; bibles were shut, swords were snatched out of their sheaths, the dropping shots told that soldiers were close upon the spot, and that in a minute or two there would be a battle. Then, the pastor threw up his hands, and cried, "Lord, spare the green, and take the ripe!" So now, when

*Mentioned by Dr Culross.

Death's troops are on us, and the alarm has been rung, we would pray, " Lord, spare the green, and take the ripe ! Take us, for whom to die would be gain ; spare those for whom it would only be loss, and this once, deliver them from this evil ! "

On the other hand, to a man whose heart is ready and whose time has come, going out of this world, is only going out of evil, and becoming in the flash of a moment sinless, sorrowless and deathless. Death means perfection for ever and progress for ever. The thing that to others would be the worst, is to Him the best. Archbishop Leighton, when once raised from a bed of sickness, which everyone thought would have been his bed of death, looked sorry, and when asked why ? said, " I thought my voyage was over, that I had done with sin, and that I was about to cast anchor ; but now, though I had reached the harbour's mouth, I find myself once more driven out to sea." If, unlike that holy man, we still feel some natural fear of the enemy, let us seek through Christ the power that will make us face our fears, that will make us do the holy right," come what may, breathing the spirit of Luther, who, as he set out at the risk of his life, to make a great confession of faith, said, " I really am afraid of Death, but there are things worse than Death, and if I die, I die."

Sin is " the evil,"—we can accept no other

conclusion. This is not because we have sympathy with many, who, while calling the Bible the standard of faith, are still apt to say, "Mind *yourself;* never mind Satan : the only Satan you have to fear is Sin." When we mark the growing tendency of men to connect the idea of Satan with comic associations, to use the name for enhancing the sparkle of festive speech, or to toss it about like a mere plaything of poetic fancy; we are marking one of the alarming signs of the times. Such triflers trifle with one of their most terrible perils. Such mutations of sacred and tremendous words we look upon with wonder, and mourn over as the sin of trifling with God's great revelations. You smile perhaps; but depend upon it, the "evil one" is a real enemy, from whom you are in real danger. He may laugh at you, but it may be death for you to laugh at him.

With all this, we hold that the present passage brings before us an evil even more terrible. "Brethren, what made the devil a devil ? Nothing but sin." So said a famous leader in the "Assembly of Divines;" and we are of his opinion. Sin is the evil that makes the "evil one" what he is. We find no evil in the world of souls of which it is not the spring. It may may sometimes look like a little thing, but it is a seed, and all the future forests of hell are in it. Sin is "damnation in its causes." It is evil in itself, and nothing but evil can come of it. If we read our instructions correctly, we are here taught to pray that we may be delivered from "the evil," not simply from one who tempts us to it. One glance at it inspires the cry, " O God, give what Thou wilt, take what Thou wilt away, but deliver us from the evil!" *

II. We shall proceed to some notes on the *Petition* for deliverance.

1. In offering this petition we have still to keep in mind *the whole connection.* Here are three prayers, all different, all in vital continuity, each having reference to sin, and one should not be offered without connecting it with the others.

* "There is no good at all in sin. First, there is no good of *Entity* or Being : God hath a Being, and everything that hath a being, hath some good in it, because it is of God : but sin is a *Non-Entity ;* a no being : it is rather the deprivation of a Being than any being at all ; and here is a great mystery of iniquity, that what is a *Non-Entity*, should have such a mighty efficacy to trouble heaven and earth. Secondly, it hath no good of *Causality:* that is, sin is so evil that it can bring forth no good. Afflictions do bring forth good. Sin is such an evil that it cannot be made good nor an instrument for good. When God brings good out of sin, he does so *occasionally*, not *instrumentally*. An *instrument* gives some efficacy towards *the effect*, but sin has in itself not even an instrumental efficacy towards a good effect, as afflictions have ; though God may take occasion to bring good out of sin committed, he never makes sin itself an instrument of good." Jeremiah Burroughs on "The Evil of Evils." 1654.

Connect this for instance, with *the prayer for forgiveness*. The "sins," also called the "debts," for which we ask forgiveness, are the formations and activities of that which is here called "to the evil." Some suppliants seem to be concerned only that they may have forgiveness, but sin itself seems to give them but little concern. Although they take deep interest in their own spiritual symptoms; they are nervous rather than penitent, and what they want is simple impunity. They will tell you that they glory in the cross, because the righteousness of Jesus there "finished," is the only righteousness that will satisfy the justice of God, and save the soul of man. They watch the Lamb of God, not as bearing away *sin*, but simply the *consequences* of sin. Like the priest of old, who in the name of the people, laid his hand over the head of the scape-goat, and ceremonially transferred their sins to it; they in fancy, put a hand on the mystic burden-bearer, and think with a selfishness that passes for Christian joy, that their sins are now clean forgiven and taken for ever out of sight. This is the one thing they seem to think of, or to care for. But just as might have been expected, in this standard prayer for the use of sinners, we are solemnly taught not only to pray for the forgiveness of sins, but for deliverance from "the evil" out of which our sins have sprung.

Connect this particularly with the prayer against *temptation*. In being taught to say, "Lead us not into temptation, but deliver us from evil," we are taught to seek that we may be led out of the way of what might tempt to sin, only that we may be delivered from sin itself. As we speak, we shudder at that thing of awful malignity, to save us from which the Redeemer died; and remember that the salvation consists not merely in remission of its penalty, but also in rescue from its power.

2. We offer this prayer that *Jesus is the medium of deliverance*. This thought must run through each successive petition from the very first. We say "Our Father" in accordance with the rule, "I am the Way, the Truth, and the Life; no man cometh unto the Father but by me." We say, "Hallowed be Thy name" through Him who says "I have declared Thy name, and will declare it." We say, "Thy kingdom come" through Him who has said, "All power is given unto Me in heaven and in earth." We say, "Thy will be done," trusting in the "Second Adam" who "quickeneth whom He will"; and who works within us to "will and to do." We say, "Give us this day our daily bread" through Him who is the "Bread of Life," and in whom we have all the promises. We say, "Forgive us our sins,"

looking for this forgiveness through His blood, according to the riches of His grace." We say, "Lead us not into temptation," trusting the high priest who was "in all points tempted like as we are, yet without sin." We say, "Deliver us from evil" through Him who once cried, "Deliver them from going down to the pit." All through the phrases of the prayer we remember Christ as the channel of its acceptance. At the time this prayer was delivered there was a necessary reticence as to the distinctive doctrines of the Gospel. These doctrines could not be fully shown until the facts on which they were founded were finished on the Cross, and lighted up by the glory of the Pentecostal day; but, revealed or unrevealed, he was, from the time when the evil came into the world, the one Deliverer.

3. This prayer specially fits the lips of christians in *a time when old sins seem to recover new power*. Long after words of Divine forgiveness have filled our souls with sovereign tranquillity unspeakable; and after Christ has given us the right to say, "Now are we the sons of God," we may find a sad need for this petition. The mystery of grace descends into us, not to change the nature of "the evil that dwelleth in us," but to fight it down, to keep it under, and at length to destroy it utterly. Whatever essence is evil once, is evil for ever.

The old nature is still the old, unconverted and inconvertible. It fights holiness to the last, so that the dying bed is often part of the battle-field, and the dying frame a castle to be stormed. Between the first day of grace and the first day of glory there may be many an alarm. Even now, we may be recalling the memory of a crisis, when the battle seemed to waver, the tide to turn, and hope to be almost lost. The most resolute soldier and most exalted saint, has had most to feel the truth of this. While perhaps one of "the saints at Rome" was mourning over the evil that still dwelt in his own heart, and saying of Paul—"Blessed man; his spirit seems to be always in heaven; what can chill his burning love, or ruffle his serene repose? Would that I could be just like him!" he who was so envied was at this very time inditing the confession, "I delight in the law of God after the inward man; but I see another law in my members, warring against the law of my mind, and bringing me into captivity to the law which is in my members. O wretched man that I am! Who shall deliver me from the body of this death?"*

The battle takes different forms and phrases. Sometimes "the evil" is practically a great spiritual dulness. We "cleave to the dust"; try as we may, we cannot rouse ourselves. We

* Rom vii. 22, 23, 24

THE SEVENTH PETITION. 249

kneel, and all on a sudden, as if our kneeling had been the signal, the mind is crowded with frivolities or crushed with cares. We speak, but we seem to speak into vacancy, prayer is mechanical as the movement of a mill, and though all our heaven depended on our prayer, we feel as though we could not pray. We try to read, but the book is a blank. We try to work, but the spirit is gone out of us. We try to realise the Unseen, we try and fail. We seem to see and hear and speak only with the body, not with the soul. The soul is in a dead calm.

"No stir in the air, no stir in the sea,
  The ship is as still as a ship can be."

This is our story, and our thought is, better the wild hurricane than the pestilential quiet. What ails us? Are we growing torpid under a spell? "Deliver us from the evil." At other times the evil within us suddenly breaks into action. Every man has some weak point on which evil is always at work, in which he is always in danger of giving way, and at which it is always possible for some evil habit to begin. One is naturally apt to be frivolous, another to be exaggerative, another to be morose, another to brag of what he has done, another to do nothing, another to be too fond of money, another of scandal, one was formerly possessed by the demon of a bad temper, "mean, contemptible, and unjust, as any of the peerage of hell." The cast out sin that was once master will be always trying to recover lost ascendancy; and though the new life loathes that besetting sin to very sickness, there is still left a nature in sympathy with it, through the treachery of which the heart may yield to it a little. With every new indulgence its demands will be more imperious, its spells more seductive; still yielding by little and little, a day may come when the man finds that his power is gone. He is surprised into a snare, and is all at once a benumbed and helpless captive, soon to wake up in the consciousness of a sorrow that drowns all the world in darkness. Though he may fall into sin, no saved man can live in it, yet he may feel as if he never could escape from it, and as if "the evil" that has now fastened on him will not be shaken off. In the oldest of all known languages, the word "throttler"—the old word for serpent, is the word also used for sin. Like the serpent in that antique marble so familiar to us—turning, twining, and clasping round Laocoon and his sons—so "the evil" twines round the soul, fastens with deadly clench, strikes to sting, and makes him cry, "Who shall deliver me?" *

* The serpent was called *ahi* in Sanskrit. The root is *ah*, or *anh*, which means to press together, to choke, to throttle. Here the distinguishing mark from which the serpent was named, was his throttling, and *ahi* meant

THE SEVENTH PETITION. 251

4. Our thoughts rush forward to the day when this prayer for deliverance from "the evil" *will have its finished and perfect answer*.

Earthly things are but poor types of heavenly things, yet they are the best we have. When we try to rise above them, and our impatient thoughts break through the shells of words, they are lost in the infinite, and we feel all about us in blank darkness; but by what comparison taken from the things of earth—the only things we now know, can we set forth the joy of this deliverance?

In the old wars between king and Parliament,

serpent, as expressing the general idea of throttler. "In Sanskrit the word meaning throttler was chosen with great truth as the proper name of sin. Evil no doubt presented itself under various aspects to the human mind, and its names are many; but none so expressive as those derived from our root *anh*, to throttle. *Anhas* in Sanskrit means sin, but it does so only because it meant originally throttling —the consciousness of sin being like the grasp of the assassin on the throat of his victim. All who have seen and contemplated the statue of Laokoon and his sons, with the serpent coiled round them from head to foot, may realize what those ancients felt and saw when they called sin *anhas*, or the throttler. This *anhas* is the same word as the Greek *agos*, sin. In Gothic the same root has produced *agis*, in the sense of *fear*, and from the same source we have *awe*, in awful, *i.e.*, fearful, and *ug*, in *ugly*. The English *anguish* is from the French *angoisse*, the Italian *angoscia*, a corruption of the Latin *angustiæ*, a straight."—Max Muller's Lectures on the cience of Language, 1862, p. 388.

the town of Taunton, attacked by Lord Goring, and defended by Robert Blake, sustained a long siege. Food rose to twenty times its market value. Half of the houses were blown down by a storm of fire, many of the people perished of hunger. Through all this, the townsfolk had been accustomed to meet in St Mary's Church to pray, and be sure that the burden of their daily prayers to the Father was, "Deliver us!" One day when assembled for this purpose, hoping to hear that the enemy had at last retreated, a trusty messenger came to the church door, and spoke but this one word, "Deliverance!" In a moment the magic word flew through the vast assembly, and all shouted with one voice, "Deliverance!"

We can understand the feeling that rang in that note. We ourselves have had many a great earthly salvation. Often and often have we had reason to sing, "our soul is escaped as a bird out of the snare of the fowler, the snare is broken, and we are escaped." We have been delivered from the grasp of death, we have been delivered from many a terrible temptation, we have been "delivered from the power of darkness, and translated into the kingdom of God's dear Son;" but we have not yet been fully delivered from "the evil." "The evil!" why it sometimes seems as if we should never be delivered from it!

When, in the course of our fight with sin, we are in the very act of exulting over some great victory, it shoots us down again, and we are gnashing our teeth in the dust. When it seems to sink in one part of our nature, it seems to rise in another. As we felt the first bliss of forgiveness, we almost thought that we had done with it for ever, and that Christ would make it as easy to be holy as it is to breathe. We felt ready to borrow the exclamation, "O my soul thou hast trodden down strength." But sin seems to be strongest when it has had its death blow. The eagle when down, strikes at you with a beak like a bolt of iron, and may flap you dead with its wing. The red deer when down, may fell you with its antlers. The dying horse may, in the plunge of its agony, break a man's limb. A harpooned whale may dash a boat over. Sin is like that. Speared through by its conqueror, it may grasp us in its last convulsions, and seem to be stronger dying than living; but we shall soon spring out from it, and cry, "Deliverance!"

All the gladness that ever lived in that word as spoken by mortal lips, will be forgotten in the glory of the joy that shall swell in the word "Salvation!" when spoken as the spirit of the prophet heard it in vision. "Lo, a great multitude whom no man could number, of all nations, and kindreds, and peoples, and tongues, stood before the throne, and before the Lamb, clothed with white robes and palms in their hands, and cried with a loud voice, saying, Salvation to our God which sitteth on the throne and to the Lamb."*

"When did I die? Am I in the body or out of the body? Is it all over? Is this real, can it be? Am I in heaven at last? Is this no bubble to snap at a touch, no dream to vanish at the cold light of day?"

After the first questions of the wakening spirit, and the cry of its first rapturous "Rabboni!" in the first flash of eternity, and the surprise of the first moment in heaven, each delivered one will deem no path to have been too steep, no trial too long, by which the spirit of God led to such an issue. The memory of the night will only brighten the miracle of the morning, and all the pains that have been fought through will enhance the blessedness of the final rest.

* Rev. vii. 9, 10

www.ingramcontent.com/pod-product-compliance
Lightning Source LLC
Chambersburg PA
CBHW060559230426
43670CB00011B/1888